TALES OF OLD BANGKOK

Rich Stories From the Land of the White Elephant

Chris Burslem

One morning, early, we crossed the bar, and while the sun was rising splendidly over the flat spaces of the land we steamed up the innumerable bends, passed under the shadow of the great gilt pagoda, and reached the outskirts of the town. There it was, spread largely on both banks, the Oriental capital which had as yet suffered no white conqueror.

Joseph Conrad, The Shadow Line, *1917*

EARNSHAW BOOKS

Tales of Old Bangkok

ISBN-13: 978-988-19984-2-2

HISTORY / Asia / China

EB059

Published by Earnshaw Books Ltd. (Hong Kong)

Acknowledgments

Creating a historical "scrapbook" like this one is far from an exact science and involves sifting through thousands of pages of old books, pamphlets, academic texts, Internet-based archives, and hastily scribbling notes along the way. We have tried to be as complete as we can in recording sources and citations, but it is possible that something has slipped through the cracks. Should you find any item lacking a citation or incorrectly attributed, please let us know so we can make the appropriate changes to future editions. We believe all items in the book are out of copyright or are included within the bounds of fair usage.

I received a great deal of help in putting this book together. I would like to thank my family, the production team at Earnshaw Books and the people of Bangkok for making their city such a fascinating, fun place to live and visit.

Chris Burslem

An Old Bangkok Chronology

Pre-1350: Bangkok a small trading centre prior to the rise of the Ayutthaya Kingdom.

1511: First mention of Bangkok in Western records by a Portuguese diplomatic mission.

1687: French establish garrison under agreement with King Narai.

1688: King Phetracha sends 40,000 men to besiege French fortress. Four months later, the French are released. Other Westerners depart Siam shortly after.

1767: Burmese sack Ayutthaya.

1768: Gen. Taksin claims throne and moves capital downriver to Thon Buri.

1782: Taksin deposed and King Yodfa (Rama I) crowned. Capital shifted across river to Bangkok.

1783: Chinese residents are evicted to make way for royal quarter; they relocate to present-day Chinatown.

1784: Emerald Buddha, "recovered" from Laos, installed at Wat Phra Kaew.

1810: Portuguese consul's arrival marks return of Westerners.

1822: First trade treaty signed with Britain's John Crawfurd.

1824: Scotsman Robert Hunter becomes first Western trader to settle in Bangkok.

1824-26: First Anglo-Burmese War.

1828: Karl Gutzlaff sets up first Protestant mission.

1829: "Siamese twins" Chang and Eng begin world tour.

1841: Cholera epidemic strikes

1844: "Bangkok Register", Siam's first newspaper, launched.

1851: King Mongkut (Rama IV) opens up trade with the West; abolishes forced labour.

1861: Europeans petition successfully for construction of Charoen Krung Road, Bangkok's first modern street.

1862: Briton Anna Leonowens hired as English teacher for children of King Mongkut.

1868: King Chulalongkorn (Rama V) ascends throne, employs Western advisers to modernise the country.
1874: Slavery abolished in Siam.
1893: French gunboats force entry into Bangkok; Siam loses provinces of Trat and Chanthaburi, and parts of western Cambodia.
1904 and 1907: France seizes Siamese areas of Laos and Cambodia.
1907: Royal family imports first fleet of motorcars.
1910: Chinese workers strike, shutting down Bangkok.
1932: People's Party stages bloodless coup against King Prajadhipok. Constitutional monarchy with a parliamentary government introduced.
1939: Country's name changed from Siam to Thailand.
1940: Prime Minister Phibul Songkhram decrees adoption of Western-style clothing and manners, bans betel chewing.

1941: Thailand declares war on Britain and the US. Japan uses Thai territory to invade Malay Peninsula, Singapore and Burma.
1942-5: Allied bombers raid Bangkok.
1945: King Ananda Mahidol returns from exile.
1947: Pro-Japanese leader Phibul stages coup, sets pattern for decades of military rule.
1949: Northern and northeastern borders closed to Chinese immigrants.
1953: New bus system introduced, paralyses traffic.
1956: Thailand bans movie "The King and I".
1959: Opium smoking criminalised.
1960: To discourage rock 'n' roll, Interior Ministry forbids bands from playing in central Lumpini Park.
1964: Thailand permits US Air Force to use bases in the Kingdom during Vietnam War; US servicemen begin to arrive in large numbers.

Kings of Thailand

Taksin Maharat (Thon Buri)	1768-1782
Buddha Yodfa Chulalok the Great (Rama I)	Apr. 6, 1782-Sept. 7, 1809
Buddha Loetla Nabhalai (Rama II)	Sept. 7, 1809-July 21, 1824
Jessadabodindra (Rama III)	July 21, 1824-Apr. 2, 1851
Mongkut (Rama IV)	Apr. 3, 1851-Oct. 1, 1868
Chulalongkorn the Great (Rama V)	Oct. 2, 1868-Oct. 23, 1910
Vajiravudh (Rama VI)	Oct. 23, 1910-Nov. 26, 1925
Prajadhipok (Rama VII)	Nov. 26, 1925-Mar. 2, 1935
Ananda Mahidol (Rama VIII)	Mar. 2, 1935-June 9, 1946
Bhumibol Adulyadej the Great (Rama IX)	June 9, 1946-present

Introduction

Royal harems, shaven-headed buddhist monks, hand-fed white elephants, twins who shared the same body, a floating city that mixed architectural grandeur with diabolical poverty . . . these were the stories that captured the imagination of the outside world and made personal accounts of Old Bangkok by writers such as Anna Leonowens (of "The King and I" fame) international best-sellers.

These tales by adventure-seekers, Christian missionaries, and colonialists would evolve into themes of exotic otherworldliness, the whim of autocratic rule, opiate-influenced hedonism, and last but not least, subjugated women that would recur over and over in the telling of the story of Bangkok well into the 20th century, when the US became the last foreign power to directly wield influence over Thailand.

The richness and lasting allure of Bangkok's story is perhaps surprising given that, up until the turn of the 18th century, it wasn't much of a place at all, acting as little more than a stop on the river to Siam's then glittering royal capital of Ayutthaya, 76km upstream.

Siam disengaged from the West early on, when French meddling in court affairs saw them expelled in 1688. Amid a wave of anti-European feeling, the British left in a hurry,

with the Dutch and other Westerners following in their footsteps. For the next century and a half, Siam's attentions were fixed firmly on the East – primarily on trade opportunities with China.

When Westerners were permitted to return in the first quarter of the 19th century, it was to a vastly different Siam. Burmese invaders had plundered Ayutthaya in 1767. The destruction was so great it was as if the Burmese had sought to bring a historical end to the Siamese, hauling away the city's population, razing almost every structure and scorching the surrounding lands.

The new capital the Europeans found in Bangkok was no match for its fabled predecessor. Only a fraction of the size, its population was made up to a large degree by Chinese traders and merchants who lived in bamboo houses on the water. It was a swampy, harsh world rife with disease, dangerous animals and pestilent insects. The royal

family sought to restore the ritual pomp and authority of Ayutthaya, reviving its architectural style and even dragging some of its ruins back to rebuild temples and palaces. But everything was to a smaller scale.

For all intents and purposes, this new capital was but a minor port in the Asian trading universe. Siam's reunion with the West was grudging, prompted by two regional wars that shook the ruling elite's view of the world. First, the British vanquished the kingdom's archenemy in the First Anglo-Burmese War. Then they humbled China, the regional superpower, a few years later in the Opium War.

When King Rama IV took the throne in 1851, Bangkok's population was less than 500,000. The first European residents described a city of many tongues and communities – Siamese, Mons, Vietnamese, Khmers, Chams, Laos, Malays, Persians, Burmese, Javanese, Bengalis, Ceylonese – but it was predominantly a Chinese-driven city and would remain so. The Chinese brought with them an entrepreneurial spirit that became a central part of Bangkok's character.

While Bangkok developed the air of a classic colonial-era port city – shipping out teak, rice, sugar and tropical goods in return for opium, weapons and other Western technologies, it nevertheless managed to maintain an independent spirit and charm that set it apart from other Asian entrepôts. There was never the large ex-patriot community found elsewhere. Even as recently as the turn of the 20th century there were fewer than 500 Westerners living in Bangkok, many working as advisers to the royal administration.

Among them were British trade experts, Belgian jurists, Scottish engineers, Italian architects, German shipbuilders and Danish military advisers. There were also those with less distinguished CVs: traders, rough-edged seamen, colonial misfits and others – like Leonowens – who were looking to reinvent themselves far from home.

Through a combination of luck and diplomatic skill, Siam emerged from the colonial period independent and more or less intact. The Kingdom developed slowly over the next half century, but always it seemed in the shadow of – or perhaps more accurately, as an afterthought to – its capital. Bangkok *was* urban Thailand. It was the seat

of power, the main market, a place of constant palace intrigue. It was where ambitious generals plotted to seize power, Cold War adversaries sparred, and where local bankers and tycoons colluded in Chinese restaurants and in the private rooms at cabarets.

Under a militaristic government led by Field Marshal Phibulsongkram, Bangkok became the capital of a newly named country — Thailand. The name change in 1939 reflected a fling with the idea of the "super nation state" and a government desire to stress the primacy of Thais above other groups, most noticeably the ethnic Chinese. One side-effect for Bangkok of this nationalistic lurch was the construction of a series of landmarks, such as the Victory and Democracy Monuments.

The end of World War II ushered in a political dark age of dictatorial rule, not unrelated to the rise of the US as Thailand's new patron. When American GIs arrived in the 1960s they found a city with a well-established and lively nightlife. Their presence, however, ensured it gained a worldwide notoriety.

While the bars, Western restaurants, rock 'n' roll and youth culture were the most obvious trappings of an increased exposure to America, US influence ran much deeper. Through its investments in Thailand's infrastructure, institutions and markets, as well as its policy input and economic

"guidance", it put Thailand on the road to becoming an Asian tiger. The great drive to development since the 1960s marked the end of Old Bangkok. The city's famous canals were nearly all paved over, many of the shop houses bulldozed and rebuilt as commercial complexes, the market gardens on the fringe of downtown redeveloped while the temple-dotted skyline yielded to one dominated by skyscrapers. The trams and rickshaws became but a distant memory.

To be sure, some things haven't changed. The city never got on top of its traffic; it's always been bad. The scrappy charm, wonky mix of architectural styles and love of street-side eating remain essential parts of Bangkok's personality. Barges still crowd the river, monks continue to do their morning rounds and elephants wander the streets in the low season. Perhaps most of all, the city's denizens have retained their distinctive easy-going manner and their love of "*sanuk*," that joy for life that has distinguished Bangkok from all other Asian capitals.

Through the words of visitors and residents, in pictures, newspaper clippings and vivid anecdotes, we have tried to capture some of that spirit. My hope is that you will enjoy discovering the past of this great city as much as I have.

Chris Burslem
October 2011
Bangkok

9

Bangkok Bound

From F.A. Neale's Narrative of a Residence at the Capital of the Kingdom of Siam, *1852*

"Holloa!" exclaimed the captain, "you here! Why what port are you bound for now?"

"That is just the question I was about to put to you myself," was my rejoinder.

"Oh, as for me," he replied, "I am bound for Bangkok, in Siam, and sail to-morrow evening if the weather permits, – a queer outlandish place it is – and if you have nothing better to do, take a trip down there with me; I'll go bound you won't repent the voyage."

"Agreed," said I; and agreed it was.

"Even matter-of-fact Singaporeans had done their best to dissuade me…'For goodness sake don't go to Bangkok,' they said. 'Bangkok is the hell-hole of the East. It is full of cholera, leprosy, and other plagues. White men's burial services are more common than heathen festivals. You'll never come out of Siam alive.' "

Andrew Freeman, Brown Women and White, *1932*

Asiatic Venice

From A Week in Siam, *Ludovic Marquis de Beauvoir, 1867*

Behind a bend of the Maenam [Chao Phraya], the entire town of Bangkok appeared in sight. I do not believe that there is a sight in the world more magnificent or more striking. This Asiatic Venice displays all her wonders over an extent of eight miles. The river is broad and grand; in it more than sixty vessels lie at anchor.

Everything You Need

From The 1904 Traveller's Guide to Bangkok and Siam *by J. Antonio*

Out of the way it may be, Bangkok is well supplied with steamers and rarely does a day pass without one or two leaving or departing. The general time taken by the direct boats from Singapore is about three and a half days. You can also travel to Bangkok from Hongkong and Saigon. Other routes to Bangkok had best be left to the explorer or professional traveller as they present difficulties which require a great deal of surmounting. As for what to bring with one, the stores of Bangkok can, as one of them proudly boasts, supply you anything from the proverbial needle to the anchor and just an ordinary outfit suited to the tropics is all that is needed.

> "Bangkok! I thrilled. I had been six years at sea, but had only seen Melbourne and Sydney, very good places, charming places in their way – but Bangkok!"
>
> *Joseph Conrad,* Youth, *1888*

Mahachai Road, one of the first modern streets in Bangkok, 1902

11

You Say 'Bangkok', We Say 'Krung Thep'

The origins of Bangkok's name are unclear. The most popular theory is that it derives from *bang*, the Thai name for a village on the bank of a river, and the shortening of *makok*, the name for a species of wild olive. The Portuguese picked up on the name *Bang-kok,* and the outside world has known the village/ town/city/megalopolis by that name ever since. When Rama I moved the capital across to the east bank of the Chao Phraya in 1782, he gave the city a ceremonial title that is recognized by Guinness World Records as the longest place name in the world:

Krungthep Mahanakhon Amonratanakosin Mahintara Ayuthaya Mahadilok Popnopparat Ratchathani Burirom Adomratchaniwet Mahasathan Amonpiman Avatansathit Sakkathattiya Witsanukamprasit.

The City of Angels, Great City, the Residence of the Emerald Buddha, Capital of the World Endowed with Nine Precious Gems, the Happy City Abounding in Great Royal Palaces which Resemble the Heavenly Abode wherein Dwell the Reincarnated Gods, A City Given by Indra and Built by Vishnukarn.

Locals call it merely Krung Thep, "City of Angels", and its official name today is Krung Thep Maha Nakhon.

Learning the Language

Like all languages, Thai is as much a living historical record as a means of communication. Part of the Chinese-influenced tonal and monosyllabic Tai family of languages spoken from southern coastal China to Assam in northern India, it borrows extensively from first the Mon, the dominant culture under the Dvarati period (6th to 13th centuries), and then the Khmer – whose language served as the lingua franca for traders, diplomats and royal courts throughout much of Southeast Asia. The language also absorbed Sanskrit and Pali words under the influence of Brahmanism and Theraveda Buddhism. As late as the turn of the 19th century, Central Thai was still a minority language within the borders of what is now Thailand, with more people speaking other Thai dialects or forms of Lao, Khmer or Malay. An aggressive push by the government through schools and administrative offices has ensured it is now spoken by more than 80 percent of the population.

Inscrutable Siamese

From The Eastern Seas *by George Windsor Earl, 1837*

We passed the high islands off Cape Liant [south of present-day Pattaya] on the 30th, and steered towards the mouth of the Meinan river, on which Bankok, the capital of the Siamese empire, is situated.

Our water barica [barrel] had been carelessly placed in such a position that the whole of its contents had escaped, and the river water being perfectly salt, we approached a small trading boat which was lying at anchor, for the purpose of procuring some of a more palatable description.

Two youths who sat near the part of the Siamese boat to which I was holding, appeared rather alarmed on seeing, by the light of the torch, that they were so near a European, and they gradually retreated, casting furtive glances over their shoulders, until they concealed themselves under the thatched covering of the boat. The men however, did not seem to care much about me, and, though maintaining the strictest taciturnity, gave us the water, on which I presented them with a red cotton handkerchief, which was received without a word of acknowledgment, and having concluded our silent bargain, we pushed off and continued our journey.

13

Royal Reserve

John Crawfurd led a British delegation to Bangkok in 1822 with the aim of improving trade conditions with the Siamese. At his audience with King Rama II, as related in Journal of an Embassy from the Governor-General of India to the Courts of Siam and Cochin China *(1828), Crawfurd waited several long minutes before the monarch addressed him as follows:*

"I am glad to see an envoy here from the Governor-General of India. Whatever you have to say, communicate to the minister, Suri-wung-koss. What we chiefly want from you are fire-arms."

His Majesty had no sooner pronounced these last words, than we heard a loud stroke, as if given by a wand against a piece of wainscoting. It was a signal apparently for the closing of the ceremony; for immediately curtains were lowered and completely concealed the king and his throne from view. A great flourish of wind instruments heralded the disappearance of His Majesty, and the courtiers falling upon their faces to the ground, made six successive prostrations. We made three obeisances, sitting upright, as had been agreed upon.

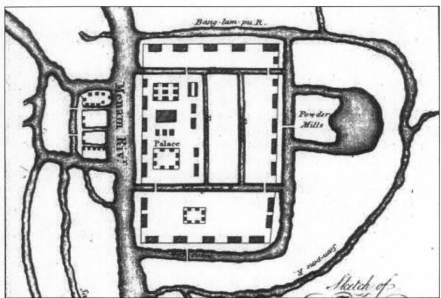

Earliest known town plan of Bangkok, published in John Crawfurd's Journal of An Embassy to the Courts of Siam and Cochin China *(1828).*

Jumbo Blunder

Norwegian Carl Bock recounting a performance in Bangkok given by Wilson's English Circus in 1880, from Temples and Elephants, 1881.

Two clowns came in and began jesting about the white elephant, claiming to own "the only genuine white animal in the world," which appeared "as white as snow; not a dark spot could be seen anywhere."

White elephants are not worshipped, but they are revered as auspicious symbols by Thai kings. This elephant was a normal grey one that had been covered in chalk powder. The Siamese were annoyed that fun should be made of their beliefs and they cursed the circus proprietor, forecasting that he would be punished by Buddha, and that the elephant would die. And their prophecy came true...The performance was, to say the least, in very bad taste.

Well-Lodged Elephant

The Dutch East India Company's Jeremias Van Vliet, 1640s

Usually the Siamese kings have one white elephant in their court, which is there well-lodged, ornamented, well treated and provided with attendants and a suite; the King often pays it a visit, and it is well fed from plates of pure gold.

The working Elephant.

15

Bigger than Bengal

In Journal of Three Voyages along the Coast of China 1831, 1832, 1833 *by Rev. Charles (Karl) Gützlaff, 1834*

Under a good government, [Siam] might be superior to Bengal, and Bankok will outweigh Calcutta. But Europeans have always been treated there with distrust, and even insolence...The general idea, hitherto entertained by the majority of the nation as to the European character, was derived from a small number of Christians, so styled, who, born in the country, and partly descended from Portuguese, crouch before their nobles as dogs, and are employed in all menial services, and occasionally suffered to enlist as soldiers or surgeons.

When the first British envoy arrived, he was treated with contempt, because the extent of English power was not known. When the English had taken Rangoon, it was not believed by the king, until be had sent a trustworthy person to ascertain the fact. Still doubts agitated the royal breast as to the issue of the war with the invincible Burmans.

But the national childish vanity of the Siamese in thinking themselves superior to all nations, except the Chinese and Burmans, has vanished; and the more the English are feared, the better is the treatment which is experienced during their residence in this country. The more the ascendancy of their genius is acknowledged, the more their friendship as individuals is courted, their customs imitated, and their language studied.

At about the same time Gützlaff was making his report, the finishing touches were being put to the imposing Wat Suthat in central Bangkok. Traditionally, stone ogres – often stylised dragons or lions – would be placed outside such a temple to repel evil spirits. This time the architects opted for carvings of Western soldiers and sailors who, to them, appeared suitably grotesque. The statues were ordered from China, and continue to stand sentry outside the Wat today.

Amazingly Quiet Thailand

From Where the Strange Trails Go Down *by E. Alexander Powell, 1921*

I was warned that the train service up the peninsula was uncertain, that the steamers up the gulf were uncomfortable, that the hotel in Bangkok was impossible, the dirt incredible, the heat unendurable, the climate unhealthy. And when, desiring to learn whether these indictments were true, I attempted to obtain reliable information about the country to which I was going, I found that none was to be had. The latest volume on Siam which I could find in Singapore bookshops bore an 1886 imprint. The managers of the two leading hotels in Singapore knew, or professed to know, nothing about hotel accommodations in Bangkok. Though the administration of the Federal Malay States Railways generously offered me the use of a private car over their system, I could obtain no reliable information as to what connections I could make at the Siamese frontier or when I would reach Bangkok. And the only guide book on Siam which I could discover – quite an excellent little volume, by the way – was published by the Imperial Japanese Railways!

The Siamese are by no means opposed to foreigners visiting their country...but, owing to the insularity, indifference, timidity and pride which are inherent in the Siamese character, they have taken no steps to bring their country to the attention of the outside world.

When one notes the energetic advertising campaigns which are being conducted by the governments of Japan, China, Java, and even Indo-China, where the visitor is confronted at every turn by advertisements urging him to "Spend the Week-End at Kamakura," "Go to the Great Wall," "Don't Miss Boroboedor and Djokjakarta," "Take Advantage of the Special Fares to the Ruins of Angkor," you wonder why Siam, which has so much that is novel and picturesque to offer, makes no effort to swell its revenues by encouraging the tourist industry.

17

Tourist Permit to See the Royal Palace, 1936

Rule 1.
Visitors must dress properly. Western dress for men must include collar and necktie. Visitors wearing knickerbockers, plus fours, shorts, blazers or sweaters will not be permitted in the grounds of the Temple of the Emerald Buddha.

Where East is Still East

By William Burton, in The New York Times, *Aug. 29, 1937*

Both white elephants and Siamese cats are virtually extinct in Siam, but the country is the most Oriental of all Far Eastern lands.

The temples of Siam are as magnificently dazzling as any dream of the Orient could be.

In atmosphere, too, Siam conforms to occidental notions of what the East should be. There is an attitude of lotus-eating languor, and any show of zeal in work that may be observed is by Chinese immigrants. The Siamese viewpoint, expressed in an old proverb, is that "in the water there is fish and in the ground there is rice" which with the sparse population means that not much is required for their simple wants. So they take life easily – and smilingly.

In another respect Siam actually conforms to the Hollywood tradition of all the Orient. There are really dancing girls there. Even in the few modern cabarets in Bangkok girls in the "floor show" still use the old native singing and hand rhythm, although often combining them with some Western foot and hip movement. It is slow and sinuous. And you can express your adoration for any given dancer by buying for a baht (about 45 cents) one of the red or white flowers in her hair. That's also an old Siamese custom.

A Jim-Crack Little Toy

From F.A. Neale's Narrative of a Residence at the Capital of the Kingdom of Siam, 1852

Paknam at the mouth of the Chao Phraya, downstream from Bangkok, served as Siam's front gate to the outside world. It had a customs office, a line of defensive placements and was home to a population of about 6,000 locals in the mid-1800s.

On a diminutive little island in the exact centre of the river rises a diminutive little white circular fortress, with a very small but beautifully constructed pagoda, towering up to a pigmy height in the middle thereof...A broad-side of ship's biscuits would almost annihilate it. Yet this jim-crack little toy is firmly believed by the king and nation to spread terror far and wide, and to be the dread of the English Government, and the only reason why they have never attempted to attack this, as they have all the neighbouring countries...Thus protected, the Siamese presume their country to be impregnable. Hence, every day, at about 1 p.m., the notes of a discordant horn resound through every town and village in the Siamese territories, meant to proclaim to the world at large, "that his Majesty, the King of Siam, had had his dinner, and was graciously pleased to grant permission to all other potentates on the face of the earth to follow his judicious example."

19

Rascally and Insolent Exactions

In Anna Leonowens' The English Governess at the Siamese Court, *1870*

MARCH 15, 1862. – On board the small Siamese steamer Chow Phya, in the Gulf of Siam....In half an hour...we came to anchor opposite the mean, shabby, irregular town of Paknam...Here the captain went ashore to report himself to the Governor, and the officials of the custom-house, and the mail-boat came out to us...The Custom-House is an open *sala*, or shed, where interpreters, inspectors, and tidewaiters lounge away the day on cool mats, chewing areca, betel, and tobacco, and extorting moneys, goods, or provisions from the unhappy proprietors of native trading craft, large or small; but Europeans are protected from their rascally and insolent exactions by the intelligence and energy of their respective consuls...A number of inferior temples and monasteries occupy the background, and are crowded with a rabble of priests, in yellow robes and with shaven pates; packs of mangy pariah-dogs attend them.

Port of Bangkok Regulation II, 1862

A vessel passing Paknam without discharging her guns and ammunition as directed by the foregoing regulation, will be sent back to Paknam to comply with its provisions, and will be fined 800 ticals for having so disobeyed. After delivery of her guns and ammunitions, she will be permitted to return to Bangkok to trade.

Four Arms, Four Legs, One Body

Scottish trader Robert Hunter arrived in Bangkok in 1824 and built the city's first brick house on the banks of the Chao Phraya. One night he saw in the river "a swimming creature that appeared to have two heads, four arms and four legs" and discovered the first "Siamese twins," Cheng and Eng – sons of a Chinese fisherman. Hunter sought permission from the boys' mother and the King to allow them to be taken abroad, and in 1829 the 18-year-olds arrived in Boston, where they quickly became a popular and medical sensation. Harvard University Prof. J.C. Warren made studies of the "ligamentous bands" that joined them and concluded "attempts at surgical separation would be hazardous and unwarranted."

The Siamese Twins

By Baron Edward Bulwer Lytton,
"The Siamese Twins", 1831

I think 'tis clear, my Twins, who ne'er
A moment could be separated,
Must almost every influence share
That e'er to either might be fated;
And little to the one or other
Could happen, not affect the brother.
And yet they were as much dissimilar
As ever Honesty and Miller are.
For me, I have the Spursheim mania,
And trace the mystery to their crania.

The Dutch in old Amsterdam do it,
Not to mention the Finns,
Folks in Siam do it,
Think of Siamese twins.
    Cole Porter, "Let's Do It", 1928

Take Your Shoes Off First

In A Voyage Round the World: Including an Embassy to Muscat and Siam in 1835, 1836, and 1837 *(1838), W.S.W. Ruschenberger recounts taking part in the first US diplomatic mission to Siam with Edmund Roberts.*

We next visited Piadadd, the captain of the port, who is also a Portuguese born in Siam. We found him in a mean bamboo hut, chewing areca nut.

He told us he had just arrived from the city with a letter for Mr. Roberts. He affected much surprise when informed that we proposed to go to Bankok.

"Very sorry – but no can go!"

"Who will prevent us?"

"Nobody prevent you – suppose you go, I tell you certain – you get me flog, and that poor old governor [of Paknam] get his head cut off!"

He urged, that the king was now well disposed towards us, and our going to the city at this time, would "break friendship." We remarked, that it was any thing but friendly to keep us so long from the city, without water or stock; for want of which, we must be in a short time suffering. He replied, that different nations had different customs. In the presence of your king, that you call President, you stand up and pull off your hat; in the presence of the king of Siam, you sit down and pull off your shoes. I am your friend. Mr. Roberts can tell you. Your laws are different from those of Siam, the same as between heaven and..." – looking significantly and at the same time pointing downwards.

I thought the comparison was just, and I suspect might be extended to the inhabitants of the two places, without a great departure from justice!

Bored Naturalist

Sir John Bowring, in The Kingdom and People of Siam *(1857), discussing the journey of German naturalist Engelbert Kaempfer.*

Kaempfer landed on the shores of Siam on the 7th of June, 1690. He amused himself, as travelers might still amuse themselves, by shooting monkeys on the banks of the Meinam; he admired the beauty of the forests, but was somewhat afraid of "the tygers and other voracious beasts," who interfered with his "simpling" [collecting herbs for medicine].

On the Menam – Styles of Native Craft.

Hard Town
From Bangkok Times, Jan. 1901

No one can fairly deny that robberies and violent assaults are much more common occurrences than they ought to be...or need be.

The farang is indeed fortunate who has not suffered from the visits of burglars; he is the exception, not the rule; while the ordinary Siamese householder lives in greater dread of the *kamoi* (thief) and *nakleng* (hoodlum) than should be the case in a well-governed town...Every dangerous character in the place is armed as a matter of right, and crimes of violence are a natural consequence.

23

Blame the Sun

In J.G.D. Campbell's Siam in the Twentieth Century, Being the Experiences and Impressions of a British Official, *1902*

In the hot regions of the earth sensual indulgence is far more prevalent, and more directly attributable to natural causes than in the colder countries of the north, and the emancipation of woman is consequently much more of an uphill task.

"In Bangkok at twelve o'clock they foam at the mouth and run But mad dogs and Englishmen go out in the midday sun..."
Noel Coward, 1929

Foreign Community

The Bangkok Calendar Magazine of 1862 gave the number of foreigners in Thailand as 102:
58 Europeans
44 Americans

Otherwise, the Place is Alright

In Eric Read's Chequered Leaves, *1913*

"Is the climate as bad as our fellow friend painted?"

"Bad? Why Lord, yes! But then every place has its drawbacks, and Bangkok's is the possession of the devil's own particular brand of warming apparatus. And the rain! When you ain't being slowly grilled at a thousand in the shade, you are sousing in floods, or the house is falling about your devoted ears in a thunderstorm…There is a filthy old river, the colour of milk-chocolate, flavoured with the juices of countless defunct and deeply lamented household pets, and one's servants consider this liquid such sacred nectar that they will wash your socks in it, and then make your tea with the same, lest any fragment be lost. Can't say I ever cared for Bangkok tea myself. Sort of personal prejudice, I suppose, but some manage to acquire the taste. Otherwise, of course, the place is all right."

"Dear me!" said the youthful Juggins, and as he was so overcome, he said it again, "Dear me."

Pomp and Circumstance

In A Voyage Round the World: Including an Embassy to Muscat and Siam in 1835, 1836, and 1837 *by W.S.W. Ruschenberger, 1838*

Desirous of conforming as much as possible to the customs of the East, on all occasions while in Siam, we were careful to appear with as much pomp and circumstance as our means would admit, and made all public visits in full dress, preceded by our band. We marched along the narrow streets to a military air, followed by a crowd, but observed none to crouch before us, as they are wont to do in the presence of the tea-kettled nobility of the magnificent kingdom of Thai.

Forever a Farang

From Brown Women and White *by Andrew Freeman, 1932*

At one of the stops several of the passengers alighted and were soon surrounded by a group of naked peasant children. They cried *"farang"* (foreigner) and touched the missionary lady's dress with shouts of pleasure. They stroked her arms and exclaimed about their whiteness. Several women, attracted by the shouting children, came up and they, too, chatted with gleeful excitement at this strange being. Their frank, carefree happiness was contagious and soon several of the passengers and the Siamese began talking, the one in English and the other in Siamese, just as if they understood each other perfectly. There was none of the cringing fear of the whites which I had noted in other Oriental countries.

To the Siamese, the foreigner is not a devil as he is in China. He is merely a *farang*, a word taken from the French *forain* to designate any white man.

The term *farang* was originally used in the Ayutthaya period (mid-14th to mid-18th centuries) for the Portuguese, essentially the only Europeans in Siam for half a century, but was later applied to all Westerners. As late as the 1850s in Bangkok, *farang doem* ("original Europeans") was still used to refer to Portuguese Christians.

Wondrous Wats

From The Gentleman in the Parlour *by Somerset Maugham, 1930*

But not...can I hope to give an impression of the surprise, the stupefaction almost, which assailed me when I saw these incredible buildings. They are unlike anything in the world, so that you are taken aback, and you cannot fit them into the scheme of things that you know. It makes you laugh with delight to think that anything so fantastic could exist on this sombre earth.

They are gorgeous; they glitter with gold and whitewash, yet are not garish; against that vivid sky, in that dazzling sunlight, they hold their own, defying the brilliance of nature and supplementing it with the ingenuity and the playful boldness of man. The artists who developed them had the courage to pursue their fantasies to the limit...they knew no reticence, they cared nothing for taste.

The United Club, Bangkok.

The Worst Snobs on Earth
From Carol Hollinger's Mai Pen Rai Means Never Mind, *1950*

I found myself up to the ears in Siamese, around the clock, growing even more confused. In no way but the very superficial did I ever understand the Thai.

No Westerner comprehends an Oriental country because he has lived there a few years. Even those who spend a decade or so in the East and who go ostentatiously native are deluding themselves they know the country.

The delusions are complete if they think they are accepted by the Asians. Orientals are the worst snobs on earth. You are called a *farang* from the first day you set foot on Thai soil, and the term will still apply, if your face is white, if you remain there a score of years.

In the most familiar situations the unfathomable will suddenly arise, a specter to confront the smug who believe themselves assimilated.

There are exceptions, but very few. There is a line beyond which the millions who are Asian sleep and eat and breed in un-American poverty and of whom the Westerner knows nothing.

Gentle Folk

From A Physician at the Court of Siam *by Malcolm Smith, 1946. Smith arrived in Bangkok in 1898 and served as a doctor to the Royal Court before leaving Siam in 1925.*

The most striking feature of the Siamese to me was that so many of them never seemed to mature. Intellectually they remained children all their lives, with all the qualities of light-heartedness, irresponsibleness and fickleness that belong to youth; delightful people to meet but to the serious-minded European, difficult to work with.

Animal Friendly

Sir John Bowring in The Kingdom and People of Siam, *1857*

In their reception of strangers (Siamese) are eminently hospitable. Buildings are erected for the convenience of travellers, and women spontaneously bring to them jars of water to appease the thirst of those who are journeying. Their religion teaches humanity to animals; in fact, the tameness of many living creatures which in Europe fly from the presence of man is observed by all strangers. I heard of more than one instance in which Siamese had quitted the service of Europeans because they were unwilling to destroy reptiles and vermin. The gardener of the French Mission was commissioned to kill the serpents he should find among the shrubs; he refused, saying, "I cannot commit murder to gain my wages." It is a not uncommon practice for rich men to buy live fish, to have "the merit" of restoring them to the sea; and on certain days, especially the 8th and 15th of the month, which are deemed holy, fishing and hunting are absolutely prohibited.

BANGKOK: "THE VENICE OF THE EAST."

"There is no medium in Siam; it is either gorgeously gilded palaces and fantastically adorned temples, or filthy-looking huts."

Capt. GJ Younghusband, 1888

"The general appearance of Bangkok is that of a large, primitive village, situated in and mostly concealed by a virgin forest of almost impenetrable density. On one side beyond the city limits were paddy fields, and on the other to the very horizon stretched the exuberant jungle."

Frank Vincent, 1871

30

High-Flying Phaulkon

Some time around 1678 a young Greek trader, Constantine Phaulkon, was shipwrecked on the coast of southern Siam and made his way to the legendary capital, Ayutthaya. Phaulkon quickly ingratiated himself with King Narai – no mean feat in a court known for secrecy, ritual and fear. He became fluent in Thai and worked at court, first as a translator and then, because of his involvement with the East India Company, a counselor to the king. He was also a friend of the French at the expense of the British and Dutch – and engineered a Franco-Siamese agreement that led to the exhcnage of numerous French and Siamese embassies.

But his support for the French Jesuit missionaries and closeness to the king aroused suspicion in the court that he intended to convert the king to Catholicism, press Western interests or even seize the throne. Phaulkon and the royal heir were both arrested and, after the death of the terminally ill king, executed by Narai's usurping foster brother. Phaulkon was beheaded with a sword; the prince was placed in a red cloth bag and beaten to death with sandalwood clubs. Europeans were not again welcome at the Court of Siam for more than a century.

"At length he was accused of designing to put the king to death by inviting him to visit the church he had built, between the walls of which, it is said, he had inserted a quantity of gunpowder which was to be ignited by a match at a given signal and thus involve the death of the king."
Henri Mouhot, 1864

Costantino PaulKon Veneziano- Dinominato il Sig: Costanzo.

31

Bare Essentials

French Jesuit priest Nicolas Gervaise in The Natural and Political History of the Kingdom of Siam, *1688*

In the kingdom of Siam there is no trade more unprofitable than that of tailor, for the common people have no need of such a man. The whole dress of a man consists of two pieces of silk or cotton material.

Clothed in Shame

George B. Bacon, Siam, The Land of the White Elephant as It Is and Was, *1892*

If all would at all times wear the native dress there would be no occasion for fault-finding. But as a nation they do not know what shame is, and as the climate is mild and pleasant, and the majority of the people poor and careless, their usual dress consists of a simple waist-cloth adjusted in a very loose and slovenly manner; while many children until they are ten or twelve years old wear no clothing whatever. When foreigners first arrive in Siam they are shocked almost beyond endurance at the nudity of the people...Not until Siam is clothed need she expect a place among respectable, civilized nations.

One or Two?

From a report in the Philadelphia Medical Times, *1874*

The exhibitions [of the Siamese twins] in England were attended by great throngs...A rather greedy young British lady became enamoured of Chang and Eng. She probably thought if one husband is good, two might be better and wanted to marry them. When told that she would end up in the dock as a bigamist she lost interest and quickly married a "heavy whiskered commercial gentleman."

Despite their immersion in show business, Chang and Eng remained basically gay, good-natured, shrewd country boys with simple wit. On occasions they were great jokesters.

Once, in a playful mood Chang and Eng boarded a train with only one ticket. Around their shoulders they wore a generous cape which concealed the connecting band. The conductor first asked Eng for his ticket. He said he didn't have one, so the conductor told him to get off the train. "Very well," said Eng. He arose to go, accompanied by his brother, "But I have a ticket," Chang protested, "and if you put me off, I'll sue the railroad."

Forsaken

In A Voyage Round the World *by*
W.S.W. Ruschenberger, 1838

The famous Siamese Twins were a theme of conversation. They have been probably of as much service as any pair of patriots in their country, first, by generally calling the attention of the Christian world towards it, secondly, by affording Mr. Bulwer a subject for his pen, and last, by causing some of the Siamese interested in them, to hear of countries of the existence of which they were ignorant before the brothers set out on their travels. "Where are the twins?" was asked of every one who visited the shore. [Port captain] Piadadd shook his head: "Their poor mother cry plenty about those boys. They say, they make plenty money – no send never any to their poor mother."

The Floating City

Joseph Conrad showing enthusiasm for the city where he assumed his first captaincy in The Shadow Line, *1915.*

There it was, spread largely on both banks, the Oriental capital which had yet suffered no white conqueror...in those miles of human habitations there was not probably half a dozen pounds of nails.

Shared Destiny

From Siamese Twins: Some Observations on Their Life, Last Illness and Autopsy *by W.B. Daniels, 1963*

Chang and Eng...became naturalized United States citizens. They took the surname of Bunker...They settled in...North Carolina near Mt. Airy, where they became competent and prosperous farmers. In 1843 they married 2 daughters of a Virginia clergyman, Daniel Yeats – Chang to Adelaide and Eng to Sarah Ann. Adelaide had ten children and Sarah Ann eleven.

As the families grew it was found necessary in the interest of peace and domestic felicity for the twins to move to separate houses about a mile apart. A firm pact was made that Chang and Eng would spend three days in one's home and then three in the other's. Chang and Eng suffered financially after the civil war, particularly as a result of the loss of their slaves... Chang and Eng soon went to Europe again under the more expert direction of P.T. Barnum. While aboard ship returning to America in 1870, Chang had a paralytic stroke during one of his increasingly frequent alcoholic debauches...thereafter, on their return to Mt. Airy, Eng carried much of Chang's weight.

On Monday, January 12, 1874, Chang complained of pain in his chest...On Friday Chang felt better, but that night he "had such severe pain..." Finally, about one o'clock they went to bed...Later Eng

awakened and asked his young son, "How is your Uncle Chang?" The boy said, "Uncle Chang is cold– Uncle Chang is dead." When his wife entered the room Eng began crying out to her, "my last hour is come, I am dying." ...The only notice he took of Chang was to move him nearer. His last words were, 'May the Lord have mercy upon my soul'."

35

Glorious Confusion

In The Eastern Seas, *George Windsor Earl, 1837*

We now threaded our way among junks, boats, and floating houses, jumbled together in glorious confusion, and totally concealing the banks from our view. Hundreds of small canoes, some not larger than clothes-baskets, were passing to and fro, many of them containing talapoins, or priests, paddling lazily from house to house, collecting presents of provisions. The occupants of the floating houses were taking down the shutters which formed the fronts, exposing their wares for sale; printed calicoes, paper-umbrellas, sweet- meats, fruits, pots, pans, &c., being placed in situations the best calculated to attract the notice of the passers-by. This occupation was carried on entirely by the women, the men being either seated on the platforms smoking their segars, or making preparations to take a cruise in their canoes... At this period of the year, when the river becomes swelled by the rains, whole streets of floating houses, together with their inhabitants, sometimes break adrift from their moorings, and are carried down the river, to the utter confusion of the shipping. These floating streets, nevertheless, possess their advantages. A troublesome neighbour may be ejected, house, family, pots and pans, and all, and sent floating away to find another site for his habitation.

Venice? More Like Rotterdam

From Five Years in Siam *by H. Warington Smyth, 1898*

But where was the Bangkok I had read of – that Venice of the East…with its gilded palaces and gorgeous temples? Before us lay but an eastern Rotterdam; mud banks, wharfs and jetties, unlovely rice mills belching smoke, houses gaunt on crooked wooden piles, dykes and ditches on either hand, steam launches by the dozen, crowded rows of native rice boats, lines of tall-masted junk-rigged lighters, and last, most imposing…British steamers, and Norwegian and Swedish barques and ships…I had yet to learn that there are many Bangkoks, and this was the port of Bangkok, the commercial and the European Bangkok, where the rice and teak are milled and cut and shipped away.

Washed with the Currents

An American missionary, 1886

A curious-looking place [Bangkok] is; for, in obedience to a royal mandate, the dwellings of the humbler classes are built on bamboo rafts in the river, the privilege of building on the banks being reserved for persons of distinction…A long line of huts stretches for several miles up the river. These are fastened by chains to each other and to the shore, and are further secured by poles driven into the bottom of the stream, so that the houses can rise and fall with the tide, without endangering the safety of their inmates.

The British Embassy

The Foreign Office in London was slow to provide funds to establish a consulate in Bangkok following the signing of the Bowring Treaty between Great Britain and Siam in 1855, so King Mongkut stepped in, ordering the appropriation of a plot of land next to the Portuguese Consulate on the east bank of the Chao Phraya River, and extending a loan of 16,000 ticals to enable Britain's local representatives to begin work on a residence and office.

The consulate was raised to the status of a legation in 1895 but Bangkok was not a popular posting for the British Empire's diplomatic foot soldiers. Following the recall of Sir Reginald Tower in 1902, the position of consul stood vacant for two years until filled through the promotion of Ralph Paget. Paget was not keen on the riverside location. He found it noisy and polluted, with the constant clanging and rattling of trams outside and the bustle of passing steamers on the river. The rice mills on the opposite bank periodically covered the mission in ash. One of the expatriate community's more notorious bars, run by an Italian by the name of Madame Staro, with the support by a stable of young ladies, was also

immediately opposite the legation.

Again the Foreign Office showed a reluctance to part with money to fund a move, and it wasn't until a March 1922 that the present site of the British Embassy was acquired from a local business tycoon, Nai Lert (who had gained fame introducing ice to Siam).

The move to what was then the outskirts of Bangkok wasn't particularly popular, especially with those involved in the shipping business or the many British subjects, such as Indians, Burmese and Malays, who had difficulty getting there because of the lack of bus or tram routes. Still, with the large proceeds from the sale of

the riverside site (now the home of the Thai General Post Office), Britain was able to build a landmark mission on 12 acres of land on Ploenchit Road. The British Legation achieved full embassy status in 1947.

In 2006, Britain sold off almost one-third of the embassy grounds, including most of the glorious front lawn, to a department store operator, the Central Group. The company's plans included a 37-storey hotel and retail complex to be called Central Embassy. The design leaves intact a large concrete pillar that once stood guard on the southeastern corner of the embassy, and which for a long-time was regarded as a marker of the outer limits of urban Bangkok.

A British Judge's Recollections of Siam

H.P. Wilkinson writes about his experience in Bangkok as the British Acting Judge in an article published in the North-China Herald, *31 October 1925.*

Going to Bangkok as British Acting Judge in 1903, the captain of the steamer said to me while steaming up the Menam River: "Do you see that place on the right: that is the cemetery. You will be damned lucky if you ever see it on your left."

That was his opinion of the climate. I then and there made up my mind, hastily perhaps, that I would rather be a living Crown Advocate than a dead Judge, and therefore, though asked to remain, I came back to Shanghai in 1905 when my father's resignation as Chief Justice of the Court here left the way open for me to resume my work as Crown Advocate, and whatever was left of the private practice.

My most interesting experience in Siam was as one of the guests of Royalty at an elephant hunt at Ayuthia, the ancient capital. This was the only occasion while in Siam in which I slept in a room. At all other times one slept in the open on the verandah. Two other of the guests and myself were put up by a village chief. The room was enormous, and there was some opening to the air, but as the night went on we were wakened by a curious penetrating Oriental odour. When light came we found that we were sharing the honour of the best apartment in the village with some of the chief's dead relations, who, in the Siamese manner, were being kept for a convenient day on which to put them on a funeral pyre.

The Siamese were kindness itself, and no better hosts at official entertainments could be imagined. The Foreign Office dance was the great social event of the year, and an invitation to it meant that the recipient moved in diplomatic circles.

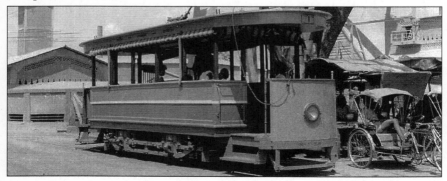

What the Police Are For

From The Straits Times, *3 October 1905*

In the British Court for Siam, the other day, before His Honour Judge Skinner Turner, a man named Francis Lanchay was charged by the Police with being drunk and disorderly and with assaulting the Police and others. [The] accused pleaded guilty, and said he was very sorry for what he had done, and that he was mad to do it. He came there looking for work, found it, and had some drink on the strength of it.

His Honour: Where did you get your liquor? — At a Chinese shop. I met a friend.

His Honour: It is a very great pity.

Mr. Gibbins (for the prosecution): I understand that he knocked the Police about.

His Honour: Of course. They always do. That is what police are for (laugher).

The case was then remanded.

THE "Bangkok Times" of the 20th ult., has the following amusing vignette of the Police Court there :—

A native of India named Appanah was brought to the British Court for Siam this morning and presented to his Honour Acting Judge Wilkinson, by Inspector Nai Nuey, together with the following letter :

" Bangrak Station.

" Sir—As Appana is too much drunk and riotous behaviour in the pubricks road. Nai Nuey, Inspector of Police. "

His Honour: Ah yes, and he was locked up all last night. Don't you think that is enough ?

Inspector Nuey : Yes, Sir.

The accused said he had been to see his friends and had had a drink given to him.

His Honour : Go away, and don't do it again. (To the Inspector) If you catch him again, just remind me of this.

And Appanah briskly left the Court.

Canal City

A Siamese belief in the importance of the head compared with the rest of the body led the royal family to claim the upstream bank of Bangkok for their palaces, temples and residences. While not a strictly hierarchical arrangement, next came the Chinese and Indian quarters in Sampheng, followed by the Europeans – a few decades later – along New Road. For the large part of the population living on the water, location wasn't a big issue. Their mostly bamboo houseboats were easy to move – even onto land. The owners simply put in columns, transforming them into tall stilt houses. However, few people wanted to be far from the river as much of early "solid" Bangkok was, by most accounts, a foul-smelling swamp, especially in the rainy season.

As the city evolved, it left its water-based origins behind. The last major klong (canal) was dug in 1895, and while a few extensions were later added, the capital's canal-building era was over by 1915. In the drive for modernity most of the canals were paved over to form roads while others, except those gracing the royal quarter, became filthy through lack of use.

Wet Sarongs

In Cities of the World: Bangkok *by James Kirkup, 1968*

When one is floating along the canals one often sees men and women and children taking a dip in the scummy water: a pretty young Thai girl descends the steps of her house, decently clad in a sarong tied tightly above her breasts instead of around the waist. Those little Thai breasts – how firm, fresh, silken they are!

Not in the Water

Proclamation of King Rama IV, 1852

By Royal Command, Reverberating like the Roar of a Lion, Be it declared to all servants of the Crown of higher and lower rank and to all the people of the Realm as follows…

His Majesty is graciously pleased to advise that under no circumstances whatsoever should any person allow himself to throw a dead dog, a dead cat, or the carcass of any other species of animal into any river or canal, whether big or small…By the exercise of a little thoughtfulness it should not be too difficult to perceive that other people using the water along the waterway do object to such exhibition. Were provincial priests from the Lao country and other northern districts or other country gentry to pay a visit to the Divine City and find the said objectionable custom still in practice, they would undoubtedly carry away the impression that conditions inside the City are not as healthy as outside it, the water supply in the City being so unclean as to breed in the dwellers thereof a number of unhappy ailments…The same or similar impressions would be given to Englishmen, Chinese and all foreign Orientals who come to do business in the Divine City…From now on should any person disregard His Majesty's gracious advice and still allow himself to practice the said inelegant habit as heretofore, he, shall…be conducted in ignominy around the City by the Nai Amphoe as a sorry object of warning to others against committing such an inhuman and irresponsible act of water pollution[.]

Waterworld

Thai poet Sunthorn Phu, 1786-1855
Sawadi Raksa
In taking a bath in the river,
You should face downstream.
The voiding of nature is
prohibited.
Do not face upstream for you
may fall victim to the black
arts.
After finishing your business,
always pay respect to Ganga,
the Water Goddess.

Monsters

Nicolas Gervaise, The Natural and Political History of the Kingdom of Siam, *1688*

In the less frequented part of the river one often encounters enormous crocodiles, which are hostile to humans and fish alike. As the Siamese cannot refrain without frequent discomfort from frequent bathing, scarcely a year passes in which some unfortunate is not devoured by these monsters.

Crocodile Charms

Sir John Bowring's The Kingdom and People of Siam, *1857*

If a person is reported to have been seized by a crocodile, the King orders the animal to be captured. The charmer, accompanied by many boats, and a number of attendants with spears and ropes, visits the spot where the presence of the crocodile has been denounced, and, after certain ceremonies, writes to invite the presence of the crocodile. The crocodile-charmer, on his appearance, springs on his back, and gouges his eyes with his fingers; while the attendants spring into the water, some fastening ropes round his throat, others round his legs, till the exhausted monster is dragged to the shore and deposited in the presence of the authorities.

Get Meds Now

An advertisement in the Bangkok Recorder, *Feb. 1845 – on the back page of Bangkok's original newspaper, written in Siamese. It is believed to be the first ad published in Thailand.*

Quinine that used to be sold at Hunter Building is now sold at my house. Since I realise many people in Bangkok have got malaria, I want to help them. I therefore offer the quinine for sale. Its owner gives me a price and I charge the price its owner gives without any profit. Now there are 40 bottles of quinine for sale. Bt17 for each bottle and get a discount if you buy all. Every bottle is the same, good quinine. Do not be curious about its quality.

Rev. Dan Beach Bradley, M.D.

My First Temple

From A Woman of Bangkok *by Jack Reynolds, 1956*

I remember my first Siamese temple, my first paddy-field full of brilliant green rice, my first wild egret, my first sarong, my first water buffalo with its enormous slate grey barrel of a body, my first huge lotus flowers, my first bare female breast and my first little Chinese boy flying a kite. Because I am I the most enduring recollection is the breast, but at the time the most impressive was undoubtedly the temple.

Wail of Death

In 1841, cholera broke out in Bangkok, killing more than 1,000 residents during the first 24 hours. Many of those who succumbed to the disease were poor immigrant Chinese who had little immunity to diseases borne by river water. For all Bangkok's allure as a floating city, disease, especially cholera (known locally as the "sudden death") was rife. Before a regular water system was established in 1914, the poor's source of drinking water was the river and canals, while foreigners and the wealthy used rainwater stored in jars. Bishop Jean-Baptiste Pallegoix, describes an 1850 cholera outbreak in Description du Royaume Thai *(1854).*

Such was the virulence of the disease on the second and third days, that relatives and connexions fled from the house infested, leaving the unfortunate victim to perish in all the horrors of solitude and unquenchable thirsts, and the priests, much against their will (although the more hardy of them laid their hands upon such booty as they found in the houses of the dead), were compelled to fly from house to house with the ostensible motive of succouring the sick and throwing the dead into the river, with weights attached to them, so as to prevent their bodies coming to the surface again before they had been floated far out to sea.

To deny that we ourselves did not share in the general panic that reigned around us, would be equivalent to an untruth. It was perhaps true that we possessed more moral courage, and more resignation to the decrees of Providence than our less enlightened neighbours, the Siamese, but it was a fearful thing to see the destruction that raged around. And it was appalling to hear the death-wail wafted over the water as ever and anon this sad signal gave notice that the messenger of death had crossed another threshold.

The Bangkok "Bowery"

From Golden Gate to Golden Sun *by Hermann Norden, 1923*

We went to the "Bowery" of Bangkok, where my friend seemed to be well-known. The "boss" ordered his henchman to take me for a look-see. As we walked through the narrow vile-smelling alleys, I did not enjoy being so tightly sandwiched in between by my roughneck escorts, but when they explained that, so walking, I was less chance of being stabbed in the back, I hugged them tight. We stumbled over filthy, slippery boards. Because of the darkness I never knew whether I was ashore or on a raft in the water. We stopped at shanties here and there, and I saw the familiar sights of opium smoking, the addicts lay in a happy stupor, forgetting their terrible world.

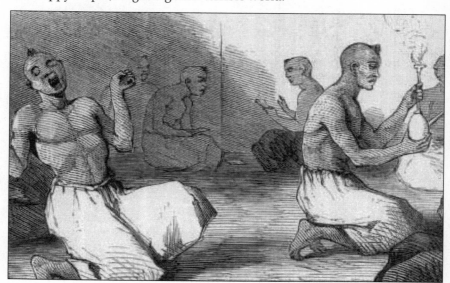

Vice of Every Vileness

Anna Leonowens describing the "Amazonian guard" watching over the king's harem in The English Governess, *1870.*

Here were women disguised as men, and men in the attire of women, hiding vice of every vileness and crime of every enormity–at once the most disgusting, the most appalling, and the most unnatural that the heart of man has conceived.

Rice and Floozies

Jack Reynolds' A Woman of Bangkok, *1956*

"Hell, don't tell me you guys are getting self-conscious about driving up to the old red lamp in a UN jeep," Boswell jeers. To me he adds, "When the Thai start to get shy about seeing floozies it'll be time for us westerners to go home – but that'll never happen," he goes on cheerfully.

"The whole economy of this country is founded on rice and prostitution. It's the floozies that keep the bloody police in pocket money."

Pantomime Police

From H. Warington Smyth's Five Years in Siam, from 1891 to 1896, *1898*

Bangkok had long been equipped with a Lord Mayor and an incompetent police force, under the Home Department, composed of all the most useless and lowest of the population, and rigged in a marvellous uniform quite in the style of a pantomime policeman.

It was chiefly remarkable for the tightness of its trousers, the size of its helmets, and the charming gradations of colour from which it passed from its original ethereal blue...The finest built man in the world would look a scarecrow in such a uniform, while the Siamese was never intended by nature for trousers.

Tough Justice

From The Kingdom and People of Siam *by Sir John Bowring, 1857*

The capital punishment of nobles is extraordinary in Siam. They are put into a sack, and beaten to death in a public place. Such, a few years ago, was the fate of the son of the most powerful noble in the land...who was supposed to have been intriguing with one of the wives of the late King...Executions are rare; beheading is the common mode of their infliction...Some offences are visited by very barbarous punishments. The penalty for melting an idol of gold or silver, stolen from a temple, is to be burnt alive. Adulterers are punished by marking with a hot iron on the cheeks, and the forehead is sometimes branded for other crimes. A bonze [monk] convicted of adultery is stripped in public of his yellow robes, flagellated till the blood springs, and condemned to cut grass for the royal elephants to the end of his days. The *ta ven* is another punishment to which particular opprobrium attaches. The convict, loaded with chains, and wearing the *cangue* [a heavy wooden collar], is marched through the principal streets of the town, preceded by cymbals and accompanied by police-officers; he is compelled to cry without ceasing, in a loud voice, "My crime is – (so and so). Be warned by my example." When his voice is weak or silent, he is beaten with swords. He is thus escorted for three successive days through the town on foot, and three times in a boat round the city, subjected to the same conditions.

The Culprit Priest's Lament

A poem reportedly composed in the 1850s by a monk who had broken the rules of celibacy.

And a fearful doom waits thee and me,
A fearful doom indeed;
Behold the faggots blaze up high,
The smoke is black and dense;
The sinews burst, and crack, and fly:
Oh suffering intense!
These all consume – the search were vain
For the lovers' mingled ashes.

> "I had heard about the executions…in which the executioner dances in front of his victim before he swings his sword. There is, I heard, always betting among the spectators whether the head will be severed at one blow or two. The executioner gets an extra fee of ten ticals if he does his work with one swing of his sword."
>
> *Hermann Norden, 1923*

Monks Among the Harem

From Journal of Nine Months' Residence in Siam *by Jacob Tomlin, 1831*

A sad disaster happening in the palace at this critical juncture, [and our] coming hither was said to be the occasion of it; Some licentious Talapoins, who swarm about the palace, had secretly got into the royal harem, amongst the wives and concubines of the king…400 of the Talapoins were put in irons. An edict was issued, prohibiting any one from receiving our books under a severe penalty… Mr Hunter was requested by the Phra Klang [Senior Minister] to take us out of the country in his ship…We are persuaded these Catholic Christians are underneath our worst enemies, and perhaps at the bottom of the whole matter.

To Die by the Sword

From The Pearl of Asia *by US Ambassador Jacob T. Child, 1892*

Having a curiosity to witness an execution I attended that of three dacoits, three of the fourteen that had been sentenced, His Majesty having commuted the sentence of eleven to imprisonment for life, a worse punishment than death. After the prisoners had been bambooed they were escorted to the ground by a squad of soldiers and police. Then their chains were stricken off and they were made to seat themselves before the crosses to which they were fastened, mud was then placed in their ears and marks drawn across their necks. The feeling of the crowd now became intense and all eagerly awaited the appearance of the executioners. The victims seemed more composed than the spectators; the head dacoit, a man about fifty years old, asked for a bogee, a Siamese cigar, which one of the attendants lighted for him and he smoked it as coolly as if he felt no terror of the fate that hung over him, that his stay on this earth was encompassed but by a few minutes; another, a magnificent young half-cast Chinaman, smiled placidly and leaned over and inhaled the perfume of the flowers placed in front of him, the other evinced some feeling. It was a strange spectacle to see those men squatting on the ground with bowed heads inside a cordon of soldiers and immediately behind them a mass of people eagerly awaiting the coming of the executioners. In about ten minutes after the prisoners were brought on the ground I observed a slight commotion among the crowd and upon looking up noticed three men enter the circle dressed in scarlet with gold fringe trimmings on their coats, each bearing a heavy shining sword; they advanced dancing and saluting with their weapons until they were immediately behind the prisoners when with a sudden whirl they struck, you heard a simultaneous thud and then saw the blood spurt upward as three bodies rose upright and fell forward, being held in place by the crosses. It seems as if death was instantaneous.

Siamese Beauties

From Journal of an Embassy from the Governor-General of India, to the Courts of Siam *by John Crawfurd, 1827*

I one day pointed out to some Siamese at Calcutta a young and beautiful Englishwoman, and wished to know their opinion of her. They answered, that I should see many handsomer when I visited Siam! La Loubère (Simon de la Loubère, who led an embassy to Siam in 1687), by his own account, exhibited to the Siamese the portraits of some celebrated beauties of the Court of Louis XIV, and was compelled to acknowledge that they excited no admiration whatever. A large doll which he exhibited was more to their taste; and a young nobleman, according to the Siamese method of estimating the fair sex, said with admiration, that a woman of such an appearance would be worth, at Yuthia (Ayutthaya), five thousand crowns!

A Woman's Burden

From The Eastern Seas *by George Windsor Earl, 1837*

The men are generally morose and unamiable, but the women are often lively and cheerful, many of them being very good-looking, although the extraordinary fashion of dressing the hair does not improve their personal appearance. Every man is obliged to serve as a soldier when called for, and to bring with him provisions for his own subsistence sufficient for his supply for several months. Wars, therefore, entail little expense on the government, which may account for the readiness with which they are undertaken. The men who are engaged in their usually inglorious campaigns, acquire habits of idleness which are never afterwards corrected, and consequently the support of these drones, and of the enormous mass of priesthood, falls entirely on the women.

Wat? Where? Why?

From Life and Ritual in Old Siam: Three Studies of Thai Life and Customs *by William J. Gedney, 1948*

The Thai *rite de passage* of life from birth to death has been inseparable from the wat. It was the desire of every Thai, from the king down to the common people, according to his means to build a wat, either individually or cooperatively, in order to gain the great merit accruing from such an undertaking. A wat is also sometimes built to commemorate great achievement or success in life. A victorious general on his return from a war must, if possible, build a wat to commemorate his achievement and no doubt to atone for having deprived a number of human beings of life, deemed a great sin in Buddhism. One may wonder why there are a number of wats left in ruins – why, instead of repairing them, people have continued to build new wat. The popular belief persisted that merit for the repair of a wat would accrue to the original owner, so that the only way to gain merit for oneself was to build a new wat of one's own.

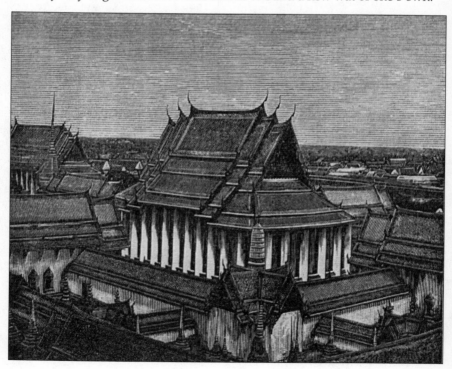

Forbidden Princesses

In Friendly Siam *by Ebbe Kornerup, 1929*

Before 1932, princesses were not allowed to marry commoners – it was marry a prince or stay single. A young commoner who fell in love with a princess, explained to a Western friend the dangers of getting too close to a princess:

"In Siam only a prince can have anything to do with a princess; for the rest of us to kiss a princess just means seven years' imprisonment and chains from neck to feet.

She also has to be imprisoned, but merely in her house alone with her maid, who has to carry the chains in a basket."

"When these delightful creatures smiled...they were repulsive. Their teeth, varnished black from the juice of the betel nut, gave their mouths the appearance of a cavern on the side of a hill."
Andrew Freeman, Brown Women and White, *1932*

The Robust Half

In J.G.D. Campbell's Siam in the Twentieth Century, Being the Experiences and Impressions of a British Official, *1902*

No one can have been many days in Bangkok without being struck by the robust physique and erect bearing of the ordinary women. It is by no means uncommon at first for a stranger, till quite close to them, to mistake them for men, the similarity of their dress and their short-cropped hair lending themselves to this deception. They do far more than their fair share of physical work.

The Fairest among Their Country Women

In A Voyage Round the World: Including an Embassy to Muscat and Siam in 1835, 1836, and 1837, *by W.S.W. Ruschenberger, 1838*

Here the Phya-pi-pat-kosa (Senior Minister), a short stout man, with a round good-humored face, clothed in a sarong of crimson silk, reclined upon a dais, in the midst of his family. Twenty of his wives were seated round *a la Turque*, with perhaps as many children. A female, resting on her knees, about two yards from the dais was fanning the minister. Thus we were introduced unexpectedly into a Siamese harem. The ladies were the fairest among their country women, I had the fortune to see; and I may add, they were graceful in their manners. They were all dressed alike, in silk drawers gathered full about the waist and ankles, and had a narrow scarf of black Canton crape thrown carelessly over the shoulders which very partially and fitfully concealed the bosom. Their bare arms were folded across the chest, showing long taper fingers, which appeared longer on account of the long-trained nails. They sat silent, and had their eyes cast down. (The ladies of the better ranks are not actually excluded from sight, but strangers are very rarely permitted to see them. They are much more comely and of a lighter complexion than those commonly met with abroad.)

"[The Siamese men] frankly admitted that monogamy seemed to them a much better marriage arrangement than theirs. Monogamy, that is, with license. Polygamy is an expensive institution and they would gladly forgo it."

Hermann Norden, 1923

The Inner Palace

Malcolm Smith recounting the closed society within the Royal Palace where King Chulalongkorn lived with his 92 wives, in A Physician at the Court of Siam, *1946.*

It was a town complete in itself, a congested network of houses and narrow streets, with gardens, lawns, artificial lakes and shops. It had its own government, its own institutions, its own laws and law-courts. It was a town of women, controlled by women. Men on special work of construction or repair were admitted, and the doctors when they came to visit the sick. The King's sons could live there until they reached the age of puberty; after that they were sent to stay with relations, or with governors in the provinces. But the only man who lived within its walls was the King.

New Ideas

From the Spokane Daily Chronicle, *30 Apr. 1932*

It is doubtful there ever will be a law abolishing polygamy in the land of white elephants, but increasing numbers of women are urging education upon Siamese women, feeling that no intelligent woman will share her husband with others...The position of No 1 wife goes to girls with money or social position. Minor wives are bought, the minimum price being about 100 ticals ($44). A girl's beauty and her father's gift for bargaining determine her price. In the household, all the minor wives become servants at the beck and call of not only of the master but the No 1 wife...For hundreds of years, Siamese women have been Lucy Stoners, custom permitting them to use either their own or their husband's name. But when it comes to private matters, until recently, they have always accepted polygamy as a matter of course. Seeing the independence of American women in the movies and observing them in person when they tour their country, has given Siamese women new ideas about themselves.

Dog Days

From The Eastern Seas *by George Windsor Earl, 1837*

It is very inconvenient to walk in the town, not only on account of the mud, but from the number of dogs, these brutes appearing to consider Europeans fair game. During two or three very short excursions in this swampy town, I was attended by two of the boat's-crew, armed with paddles, and we were therefore enabled to keep these troublesome animals at bay.

Icecream Seller, Bangkok (Siam)

APRIL – This month is the hottest month of the year...The month, being the time when the monsoon changes, is generally not as healthy for Europeans and Americans as the five months preceding, and bowel complaints prevail.

Bangkok Calendar 1862, *American Missionary Association*

Caveat Emptor

From The Kingdom of the Yellow Robe *by Ernest Young, 1898*

A fisherman one day visited a small party of Europeans who were encamped in his neighbourhood, and offered to sell them an animal for food. The creature had neither head, feet, nor tail, but their absence was explained by the vendor, who said he had removed them in order to save the white men trouble. He further stated that the animal was a hare he had trapped in the jungle.

None of the party knew very much about anatomy, but they felt rather dubious as to the truth of the man's statements. One of them, quite thoughtlessly and casually, observed, "Perhaps it is a dog."

A broad grin spread over the wily fisherman's face, for the stray shot had hit the mark. He retired roaring with laughter, and exclaimed in the vernacular, "Master very clever, very clever!"

57

Monarch Absolute

From A Physician at the Court of Siam *by Malcolm Smith, 1946*

From all his subjects King Mongkut (Rama IV) demanded absolute and unquestioning obedience...Every person in a lower station had to prostrate themselves on the ground before those in station above them, and to maintain that posture as long as they were near...The origin of the custom goes back to the early days of the people and King Mongkut did little to change it.

He took the first step in the right direction when he encouraged the people to come out of their houses and see him as he passed by...None but the Europeans are allowed to stand erect; but Siamese subjects may kneel down and have a fair sight of the King. Mongkut did most of the talking. No one could speak until addressed by him.

About 9 o'clock in the evening he went to his private apartments, and immediately afterwards his domestic bulletin issued. It named the women whose presence he desired and also those whose turn it was to be on duty through the night.

The Law of the Land

In A Voyage Round the World: Including an Embassy to Muscat and Siam in 1835, 1836, and 1837 *by W.S.W. Ruschenberger, 1838*

The government is a despotism of the most absolute kind. The King is the god, the law of the land, and his name is known only to few, that it may not be taken in vain. He is mentioned by several epithets which are considered peculiarly soft and flattering; as, "The Sacred Lord of Heads" – "The Sacred Lord of Lives," – "The Owner of All,"–"Lord of the White Elephants"–"Most Exalted Lord, Infallible and Infinitely Powerful." Even members of his body are designated in adulatory terms; his feet, hands, nose, ears and eyes are never mentioned without the prefix of Lord, or Sacred Lord. Every thing belonging to or attached to his Majesty's person is also styled golden. To visit him, is to come to his Magnificent Majesty's golden feet – to speak in his golden ear, &c.

Conversing with a King

Communication between the king and his court was often through the most stylised language and actions of total obeisance. In Grammatica Lingua Thai, and Description *(1854) a monk tells how the king's orders to a prostrate official would have proceeded:*

"The order of the most merciful King having descended upon the hairs and the head of Saraphet Phakdi, his Majesty said:

King: Mr. Saraphet! Get a ship ready; take merchandise from the royal warehouses, and fill the ship.

Page: My august lord! I receive your orders on my hair and my head.

And the official worshipped, and crawled away. He examined the ship, which he manned and loaded with merchandise, and returned to the court, and worshipped, saying –

Page: I supplicate by the power of the dust of your feet which cover my head, the slave of the Sovereign has loaded the ship.

King: With what?

Page: My august lord! I receive your orders; I have loaded three hundred piculs of cardamums.

King: What besides?

Page: August lord! The hair of your head has also shipped thirty thousand piculs of pepper.

King: Any sapan-wood?

Page: My august lord! There is sapan-wood.

King: When is she to sail?

Page: My august lord! I receive your orders; she will be ready on the 13th day of the moon.

Whereupon the official would have retreated on his hands and knees, backwards, eyes to the ground, from the royal presence.

And the Lord Sent his Teapot

Comment by US consul Townsend Harris, 1856

I am told there are five inflections or tones on each word in Siamese, and that while in sound there is but a very small difference, in sense there is a large one. I am also told that the word for angel and teapot is the same, and the difference of meaning is produced by the delicate inflection.

A missionary preaching to a Siamese audience was horrified at hearing his congregation burst out into the most uproarious laughter. On demanding the reason he was told that he had said, "And the Lord sent his teapot unto Joseph" in place of "sent his angel."

King's English

The following is a "thank you" letter from King Mongkut (Rama IV) to Britain's Queen Victoria. The king was a keen student of English and the first Asian monarch to achieve spoken fluency.

We on this occasion have liberty to let our native photographers take the likeness of ourselves when we adorned with the watch decked with diamonds and the double-edged sword which were honorary royal gracious gifts from your Majesty, received by us a few years ago and seated ourselves by the tables containing the gift silver inkstand and desk together with the revolving pistol and rifle wholly being royal gracious gift from your Majesty.

61

The Devil in the Details

From The English Governess at the Siamese Court *by Anna Leonowens, 1870*

One night, a little after twelve o'clock, as he [King Mongkut] was on the point of going to bed...his Majesty fell to thinking how most accurately to render into English the troublesome Siamese word *phi*, which admits of a variety of interpretations.

After puzzling over it for more than an hour, getting himself possessed with the word...and all to no purpose, he ordered one of his lesser state barges to be manned and despatched with all speed for the British Consul.

That functionary, inspired with lively alarm by so startling a summons, dressed himself with unceremonious celerity, and hurried to the palace, conjecturing on the way all imaginable possibilities of politics and diplomacy, revolution or invasion. To his vexation, not less than his surprise, he found the king in dishabille, engaged with a Siamese-English vocabulary, and mentally divided between "deuce" and "devil," in the choice of an equivalent. His preposterous Majesty gravely laid the case before the consul, who, though inwardly chafing at what he termed "the confounded coolness" of the situation, had no choice but to decide with grace, and go back to bed with philosophy.

Anna and the King

Anna Leonowens (1834-1915), a British widow, was hired by King Mongkut to serve as an English teacher to the royal children. The employment of Anna as a teacher, not as a governess, was part of his attempts to modernise Thailand. Her two memoirs, *The English Governess at the Siamese Court* and *The Romance of the Harem*, were best sellers in America and Britain, although they contained many errors. The main error was to put across she came from an upper class family in Britain, the second that she was fluent in Thai, and the third that in her descriptions of King Mongkut, she used words like 'barbarian and despot' when every other foreigner who met King Mongkut found him a most remarkable man. Her tendency to play liberally with the truth was especially the case for the second book, which strings together stories from all over Asia into a tale of Oriental women oppressed by male lust.

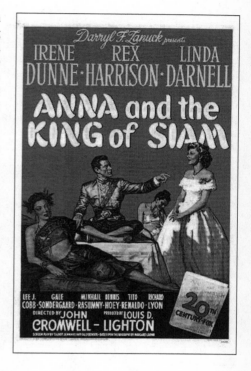

The four movie versions of Leonowens' life were largely based on *Anna and the King of Siam,* a book by a former American missionary, Margaret Landon. The first, made in 1946, oddly featured the very Western Rex Harrison as King Mongkut. The more successful, better known musical version, "The King and I" (1956), became a theatrical evergreen. It was scored by Richard Rodgers and Oscar Hammerstein and starred Yul Brynner (who won the 1957 Oscar for best actor) and Deborah Kerr.

Bangkok is one of the few cities in the world where *The King and I* has never been legally screened. The official reason provided for the ban is public disapproval of the way in which the movie portrayed the monarch. If we accept that Anna lied about her childhood and upbringing and about her time in the Royal Thai court we are still left with something wonderful – a detailed account of life in the Thai court over a period of six years.

Shall We Dance...?

Although his subjects may not have seen "The King and I", the present king has – as he told an interviewer for BBC Radio.

King Bhumibol: "I have seen it (on Broadway). As a musical comedy, or musical film, on that criteria it is very entertaining, very well done and very lavish, good musical comedy – deserved the success. But on another criteria, if we look at it as a character, the character of King Mongkut – in that movie he is a sympathetic character. He is a wonderful fellow – intelligent, strong and perhaps nearer the truth than in the original book even. My great grandfather had a very strong character. He did not dance up and down the scene – he did have a very strong sense of duty to the country."

"Every Siamese is bound to devote one-third of the year to the service of the King. This is but an exaggeration of the corvee or statute labour of the middle ages. Besides the Siamese, there are Laos, Cambodians, Burmese, and other races who have been subjugated in war, and who are absolute vassals to their masters, or to the sovereign."

Sir John Bowring, 1854

Leading from the Rear

From Description du Royaume Thai ou Siam *by Jean-Baptiste Pallegoix, 1854*

The retreat of a Siamese soldier before the enemy without the orders of his chief is punishable with death. The position of a general is understood to be behind, and not in front of, his troops. A story is told of a late commander-in-chief who had a long lance, with which he was in the habit of "pricking" his troops in their hinder parts, shouting loudly, "Forward, my children! Forward!"

To the Victors

Lao King Anouvong was captured by the Siamese in 1828 after leading a failed rebellion against Siamese rule. He was taken to Bangkok in a cage for all to see, as recounted by Jacob Tomlin in Journal of Nine Months' Residence in Siam, *1831.*

Captain Coffin saw the old king of Laos in the cage a few days ago. He seemed low spirited but calm, and addressed a few words to Captain C., saying the king of Siam had formerly behaved very well to him, and had received him in a very respectful manner when he formerly came to Bangkok...

[Two days later]

The old Laos king is dead, and has thus escaped the hands of his tormentors. He is said to have pined gradually away, and died broken-hearted! His corpse was removed to the place of execution and decapitated, and now hangs on a gibbet by the river side, a little below the city, exposed to the gaze of every stranger entering the country, and left a prey to beasts and birds.

65

Women in Chains

In A Voyage Round the World: Including an Embassy to Muscat and Siam in 1835, 1836, and 1837 *by W.S.W. Ruschenberger, 1838*

We accompanied the prince on shore, and as we walked to the palace gate, every native we met fell on his face till Momfanoi [a prince] had passed. Within the walls we found, every where, evidence of the master's tastes. A number of people, male and female, were at work, some twisting or "laying-up" rope, and others at various occupations. Several of both sexes had chains on the arms and legs and their naked backs bore recent marks of the bamboo. It was the first time I had seen women in chains, and I felt a sudden recoil of mind at the sight, of mingled disgust and pity, and perhaps, a desire that they should be at once free; but on reflection, I suppose it was correct, for they are not of the same comparative feebleness of body as in Christian lands.

One British visitor commented that although slaves, these people were often better treated than servants in England and France – proved by the fact that whenever they were emancipated, they often sold themselves back into service.

A New Order of Things

Sir James Brooke, the first White Rajah of Sarawak, in a letter to his uncle, Maj. Stuart, 1855

"Siam is, however, a country well worthy of attention, and in commercial point of view, second only to China, but the government is as arrogant as that of China, and the King [Rama III], in comparison, is inimical to Europeans... We may wait till the demise of the King brings about a new order of things. Above all, it would be well to prepare for the change, and to place our own King on the throne."

Bangkok. Wat Rachabopit.

The Lost City

From The Otago Witness *(New Zealand), 1894*

Affairs do not seem very happy in Siam. As review articles written some time ago predicted, France is badgering and will no doubt – in the interest of civilisation of course – take successive bites of coveted territory until England and France have their boundaries co-terminous.

[Bangkok] contains about 40,000 inhabitants of whom 12,000 are priests in charge of hundreds of wats (temples). It is pre-eminently a place for mosquitoes, smells, Chinese pawnshops, wild dogs – the mangy curs are never touched by the timid and superlatively lazy native priests and an agglomeration of police made up of dwarfs shrivelled up like mummies and robbing, as far as size and appearance goes from the cradle and the grave.

The dead poor are thrown promiscuously in heaps outside the town boundary, and vultures, hogs and dogs wait ravenously for the corpses.

The gaols are crowded with prisoners and now and then an attempt to escape results in the decapitation of a few as a warning to others.

Side by side with the electric tram are the ricksha, garry and bullock cart of the East. These are a few of the points of interest striking a foreigner on entering the city.

VICE KING'S LETTER TO HIS EXCELLENCY TOWNSEND HARRIS

Envoy Plenipotentiary of the U.S.
Am. to Siam, &c.
DEAR SIR:
It affords me pleasure to welcome you and your suite to our country. Please accept the accompanying fruit.

I am anticipating the pleasure of seeing you in due time, of which you shall be informed.

With best wishes for yourself, and the gentlemen of the Steamer, believe me,

Yours truly, P. S. PHRA PIN KLAU CHAU YU HUA.
Second King of Siam, &c.
Palace of the Second King,
Bangkok, Siam, April 22nd, 1856.

Keeping the Brits at Bay

The Siamese initially welcomed Britain's 1826 victory over their traditional enemy, the Burmese in the First Anglo-Burmese War. But the bitter two-year war also underscored the military prowess of the West and the European powers' hunger for territory and trade routes. By the 1830s, Britain had established bases in Malaya and Singapore, seized big chunks of Burma and subjugated mighty India, the source of much of Siam's cultural heritage. Meanwhile, France had taken control of Indochina. The colonialists had arrived at Bangkok's doorstep, casting admiring looks at its riches.

> "Two gun brigs would destroy the capital, without the possibility of resistance from this vain but weak people."
>
> *Sir John Crawfurd, 1822*

Siam's Trade in 1867

IMPORTS	EXPORTS
1. Opium	1. Rice
2. Chinese cigarettes	2. Pepper
3. Tea	3. Chilies
4. Chinese cooking oil	4. Ginger
5. Wheat flour	5. Sesame
6. Chinese preserved garlic	6. Palm sugar
7. Cannon	7. Areca nuts
8. Sword bayonets	8. Sweet zallaca
9. Guns	9. Sago
10. Iron slings	10. Corn

IMPORTS — Others: Beer (15), blue working shirts from Prussia (17), umbrellas (49), windows (68), paper (70)

EXPORTS — Others: Shark fins (20), mangrove bark (38), rhinoceros leather (55), leeches (64), tiger bone (69)

21-Gun Gaffe

From Narrative of a Residence at the Capital of the Kingdom of Siam *by F.A. Neale, 1852*

A very ludicrous incident of this description occurred whilst I was at Bangkok. The "Sir Walter Scott," one of his Siamese Majesty's sloops of war, happened then to be commanded by a rather hare-brained Irishman. Returning once from a cruise off the west coast of Cambogia, and sailing majestically up the river, wind and tide in favour, towards her moorings off the palace, and passing Mr. Hunter's house, where the British flag was proudly waving…she hove back her sails all of a sudden, and fired a salute of twenty-one guns; this happened at about one p.m., when most of the inhabitants are generally taking a siesta. The effect was most electrical, before the echo of the last gun had subsided, the river was thickly dotted with canoes, flying in all directions, and running into each other, and causing a hundred other mishaps in their confusion. As for the old King, his fear only exceeded his rage; it was with the greatest difficulty he was prevented from inflicting a very summary vengeance on Captain M—, viz., that of having him sent out of the kingdom at a minute's warning. Mr. Hunter, however, who was one of the peers of the realm, succeeded in assuaging his wrath.

The "English" Fleet

Siam's Bangkok-based navy as of 1846 included the following vessels: *Conqueror, Victory, Caledonia, Good Success, Sir Walter Scott* and *Ariel.* That most of the vessels carried English names was due to the whim of Scottish trader Robert Hunter, who had been asked by the Siamese court to help name the ships.

"I have a large fleet at my disposal, but I would rather visit you as a friend."
Sir John Bowring writing to Rama IV, 1855

Easy Money

Captain Thomas Miller and his partner C.G. Allen jointly owned the steamer Jack Waters, *which, with a large fleet of barges, plied between Bangkok and the outer bar at the mouth of the Chao Phraya. The* Jack Waters *"was the pride of the whole river fleet", according to Miller in* Over Five Seas and Oceans: From New York to Bangkok, Siam and Return *(1894).*

We were all busy, night and day, for eight months. Made money hand over fist, so that I paid [all the] debts, paid for a whole new set of machinery, paid for 14x20-inch engines and boilers...$6,000. Built a dock to haul vessels in for repairs. Built a wharf, blacksmith shop, hospital, carpenter shop, and built a new lighter, 110 feet keel, 20-feet beam, 10-feet depth of hold, to carry 3,500 piculs of rice, 206 tons, and built a coal shed and put in it 300 tons of Swansea coal at $10, $3,000. I did all this in fourteen months, and had in hand about $4,000...I omitted to say that I sent [my partner] drafts while at home, amounting to about $3,000.

Energetic Action in Closing Spirit Shops

From The New York Times, *"United States Licenses in Siam", Aug. 17, 1878*

Paris, Aug. 16. — Mr D.B. Sickels, Consul of the United States at Bangkok, Siam, writes as follows to a friend here:

"I am happy to inform you that I have finished my liquor raids, having closed over 300 establishments formerly under American protection through licenses sold by my predecessor. To-day there is not a single sprit shop within my consular jurisdiction."

Man of Many Tongues

The resume of Sir John Bowring, Britain's principal trade negotiator, was an impressive one: political economist, traveller, writer, advocate of decimal currency, instigator of the Second Opium War and fourth governor of Hong Kong. Bowring claimed to be familiar with 200 languages and could speak 100 – which helped him seal this vital deal with Bangkok, as described in Henri Mouhot's Travel in the central parts of Asia (Siam) Cambodia and Laos *Henri Mouhot, 1864.*

Great Britain and Siam remained estranged until the English Government, desirous of establishing relations with the Eastern Monarch, despatched Sir John Bowring to Bangkok with instructions to establish a commercial treaty which he effected in 1855. It was particularly from his acquaintance with the language and manners of the nation that Sir John Bowring acquitted himself so well of the task.

He was received at the Court with great favour and had several interviews with the king...the Crown of Siam consented to the appointment of a British consul at the capital, and granted entire liberty of commerce to English merchants in all maritime districts of the empire.

All duties were lowered; those upon opium almost entirely abolished, provision being made that this article should only be sold to parties licensed by the Government. On the other hand, English traders might purchase all the productions of the country directly from the producer...English subjects are permitted to settle at Bangkok[.]

Poppy Power

From Singapore Jottings *by D.I.N., 1885*

When World War II broke out, the government's monopoly on opium was still an important source of revenue for Bangkok. Losing access to Indian sources of the drug threatened this funding. The Thai military regime prevailed on its Japanese "allies" to give it control of the Shan states in northeastern Burma, an area it had identified as perfect for poppy cultivation. Just two years later, the country was forced to return the territory to British Burma, but the seeds had been sown for the rise of the Golden Triangle as one of the world's major drug-producing areas.

Chasing the Dragon

From Narrative of a Residence at the Capital of the Kingdom of Siam *by F.A. Neale, 1852*

The more opulent among the Siamese merchants and the nobles and independent men of Bangkok, are strongly addicted to gambling and smoking opium. One old, inveterate opium smoker told me, that if he knew his life would be forfeited by the act, he could no more resist the temptation than he could curb a fiery steed with a thread bridle...However true all this may have been, however ecstatic the enjoyment, — the tremulous voice and palsied frame — the deep-sunken, glassy, unmeaning eyes, spoke volumes as to the direful effects of the system.

Unwilling and Unable

From Bangkok Times, 14 Mar. 1923

Siam frankly told the Red Cross Conference that she was not at present prepared to do more towards completing her avowed policy in regard to that drug (opium).

The points taken were three: (a) the inability, through the lack of fiscal autonomy, to raise revenue to take the place of the opium revenue; (b) the difficulty caused by the smuggling of opium from other countries, which would make suppression here valueless; and (c) the want of control over the illicit sale of opium by foreign subjects, due to extra-territorial jurisdiction.

Dining Out

In Hermann Norden's From Golden Gate to Golden Sun, *1923*

Tea was served. Some passed it by in favor of Scotch. Others reclined on coaches, and enjoyed a whiff or two of opium, which had been deftly rolled into pellets by the Cantonese sing-song girls, passed through a flame and dropped into the pipes of the lotus-loving friends. Though the women all had cigarettes, I did not see any of them smoke opium, I fancy it is not done.

The Last Great Den

Richard Hughes in The Wall Street Journal, *Feb. 26, 1959*

For sale: 10,000 opium pipes with pink ivory mouthpieces, many fashioned of choice mountain mandarin wood with reputedly great curative powers over digestive disorders. Prices: Up to $100 each.

Such an ad hasn't appeared yet in the newspapers of this land of golden temples and wandering priests but it may soon. The most likely sponsor of such an ad would be Mr. Fook Chee, night manager of the world's largest opium den, the Heng Lak Rung.

Field Marshall Sarit has ordered the hundred or more opium dens in Thailand to close up by June 30.

The drive, it is readily conceded by observers here, could easily run into trouble. Twice in the past Thailand has backed down from opium-smoking bans.

Complicating things is the fact that the Bangkok police for many years have devotedly protected the opium dens. The Siamese still chuckle over the recent capture by Marshal Sarit's soldiers of a senior police official as he serenely drifted down the Mekong River piloting a raft loaded with 10 tons of illicitly imported opium.

There is no sign on the innocent-looking entrance to the Heng Lak Rung, which has a registered capacity of 8,000 smokers. It nestles next door to an ancient Buddhist temple on the hot, bustling New Road and appears from the street to be only a small

restaurant.

But above the restaurant are four spacious floors, each a crowded maze of partitioned cubicles. In these quiet, poppy-scented labyrinths, customers enjoy an average of 10 pipes apiece nightly at a cost of about 10 baht, or 50 cents – often more than a quarter of a day's wages.

Five thousand coolies use the den as their home – sleeping, eating and bathing on the premises. They leave in the morning for work, return in the evening, gulp a meagre meal, perhaps gamble and talk for a while and then, lulled by a couple of hours of unhurried smoking, fall asleep on the plain wooden floors of their cubicles.

"These unhappy coolies escape from their brutish world over their few pipes here," says a Bangkok doctor, who readily concedes that the practice shortens their lives. "Opium makes them gentler, kinder, happier." He predicts the coolies will turn to heroin with its more violent effects when the ban is enforced.

Schooling in Siam – New York Style

"A Normal College Opened in Bangkok on The New-York Plan", The New York Times, *Aug. 14, 1879*

Some time in the Spring of 1878 an article, with illustrations, was published in the *Harper's Monthly Magazine*, upon the educational system of this City, and more particularly the Normal College. In due course of time the magazine fell into the hands of the King of Siam, and so much interested was he in the article in question, that he caused the Rev. Samuel G. McFarland, a Presbyterian missionary to Siam, who he had appointed Superintendant of Education for his Kingdom, to write to Mr. Wood, President of the Board of Education of this City, for further details in regard to the college, stating that the King of Siam had resolved to civilize his people upon the same plan as that adopted by the Emperor of China, by educating them.

Mr. McFarland enclosed a check for $20, with a request that the money be invested in educational books and the books forwarded to Siam. Mr. Hood procured the books and sent them, and the check also, to the Rev. McFarland.

The books arrived in course of time, and were duly presented to his Majesty. Mr. Wood received a letter from the brother and acting private secretary of the King, acknowledging receipt of the books and thanking the authors in the King's name. The letter from the King's private secretary is written on a large sheet of unruled white paper, and is surrounded by a heavy black border, in token of the deep grief of his Majesty over the death of a royal half-brother, which occurred a few days before the letter was written. The letter of the Rev. McFarland states that a normal college has been opened in Bangkok, on the plan of one existing here; that they made arrangements for the accommodation of 80 pupils, but that about 130 had presented themselves, among whom 12 were princes of the realm and that the prospects of the success of the college were very encouraging.

Wat Mischief

Comment from a US missionary, 1886

A teacher of a Bangkok school need have little trouble with its government if it were not so impossible ever to be sure of the truth. When a boy gets into mischief, he always plans to tell a lie about it; and he can do it with such an air of candour that he will make the teacher almost disbelieve his own senses. But this fault is due largely owing to the early training in heathen homes and in the old-fashioned 'wat [temple] schools' of the country.

Solid Water

Ice first appeared in Siam as an import from Singapore in 1866 or 1867, while King Rama IV was on the throne. Prince Damrong Rajanubha later wrote that ice was among the "uncommon things" that were brought to Bangkok by steamboat.

It seems that ice was recently made in Singapore and it was offered to the King of Siam. The ice was sent in a big box covered with sawdust. The King always gives high personages and officers the ice. I and other children my age, having seen ice only for the first time, prefer to break it into small pieces and place it in our mouths, tasting its coolness for fun.

Elders seem to not like it. They complain it gives them a toothache. And there are elders who don't believe the King gives his men water ice. They say – how can we create a solid object from water?

Bangkok Golgotha

From The English Governess at the Siamese Court *by Anna Leonowens, 1870*

Watt Sah Kate, the great national burning-place of the dead. Within these mysterious precincts the Buddhist rite of cremation is performed, with circumstances more or less horrible, according to the condition or the superstition of the deceased...None but the initiated will approach these grounds after sunset, so universal and profound is the horror the place inspires, – a place the most frightful and offensive known to mortal eyes; for here the vows of dead men, howsoever ghoulish and monstrous, are consummated. The walls are hung with human skeletons and the ground is strewed with human skulls. Here also are scraped together the horrid fragments of those who have bequeathed their carcasses to the hungry dogs and vultures, that hover, and prowl, and swoop, and pounce, and snarl, and scream, and tear.

The half-picked bones are gathered and burned by the outcast keepers of the temple (not priests), who receive from the nearest relative of the infatuated testator a small fee for that final service; and so a Buddhist vow is fulfilled, and a Buddhist "deed of merit" accomplished.

(Tawny) White Elephants

White elephants, while not worshipped, have historically been seen as sacred. They signified celestial approval of the state and its ruler, and thus necessitated attentive care. Tales of pampered pachyderms astounded Europeans and led to the myth that being forced to care for one could bring financial ruin. "White elephant", too, was a bit of a misnomer; the animals are actually closer to tawny. Determining the "whiteness" of an elephant required examiners from the Bureau of the Royal Household to conduct exhaustive testing. After an elephant was certified, it automatically became property of the king.

Wild ele
Ajuth

White elephant – noun, a possession that is useless or troublesome (entered the English language in 1607)
ORIGIN: From the story that the kings of Siam gave such animals to courtiers they disliked, in order to ruin the recipient by the great expense incurred in maintaining the animal

Oxford English Dictionary

Elephants for Uncle Sam

As a gesture of friendship, King Mongkut sent gifts to US President James Buchanan in 1861. In an accompanying letter, the king said he had heard the United States had no elephants. He offered several pairs of the animals, which he said could be "turned loose in forests and increase till there be large herds." The letter, written just before the US Civil War, took months to arrive in Washington, DC; by the time it did, Buchanan had left office. His successor, Abraham Lincoln, is said to have wondered how the elephants could be employed, unless it was "to stamp out the rebellion." Nevertheless, Lincoln responded to the offer in a letter dated 3 February 1862. Lincoln politely declined the elephants, explaining the geography and climate of the United States do not "favor the multiplication of the elephant."

Great and Good Friend: I have received Your Majesty's two letters of the date of February 14th, 1861.

I have also received in good condition the royal gifts which accompanied those letters – namely, a sword of costly materials and exquisite workmanship; a photographic likeness of Your Majesty and of Your Majesty's beloved daughter; and also two elephants' tusks of length and magnitude such as indicate they could have belonged only to an animal which was a native of Siam.

"Her eyes, complexion, and above all her bearing are those of a beautiful and majestic white elephant."

Siamese envoy, after an audience with Queen Victoria, 1892

George Washington, Prince of Siam

From Malcolm Smith's A Physician at the Court of Siam, *1946*

Prince Itsarate, who was chosen by Mongkut to be his Vice-King, was his younger brother by four years. He held very democratic views on government. His greatest hero was George Washington, and in a flush of enthusiasm called his eldest son after him. When Chulalongkorn became King, Prince George Washington was made Second King, but having none of his father's fine qualities failed completely to live up to his name. He died in 1885 after which the office of Second King was abolished.

Ant Eaters

In A Voyage Round the World: Including an Embassy to Muscat and Siam in 1835, 1836, and 1837 by W.S.W. Ruschenberger, 1838

About three o'clock P. M. the table was spread in the Anglo-Asiatic style, – a mixture of English comfort and Eastern show; – the dinner was remarkable for the variety and exquisite flavor of the curries. Among them, was one consisting of ants' eggs, a costly and much esteemed luxury of Siam. They are not larger than grains of sand, and, to a palate unaccustomed to them, not particularly savory – they are almost tasteless. Besides being curried, they are brought to table, rolled in green leaves, mingled with shreds or very fine slices of fat pork. Here was seen an ever-to-be-remembered luxury of the East. Two slaves stood waving fans behind the Prince's chair, and many other attendants were crouched upon elbows and knees around the room, to whom he occasionally translated such parts of the conversation as he thought would interest them. As he thus sat, conversing cheerfully, circulating his choice wines, accurately cooled, and entertaining his guests, a slave was beneath the table, busily occupied the while, scratching His Highness' naked shins.

81

The Social Circuit

John Barrett, ex-Minister Resident and Consul General to Bangkok, in The New York Times, *July 4, 1901*

Nobody dines alone. You either invite or are invited. Invitations go out a long time ahead and there is no let up even in the hottest months, for the omnipresent punkahs and electric fans keep the diners cool.

The regular dinner hour is at 8 o'clock and it is the chief meal of the day. Fully two hours are spent at the table before the ladies go out on the veranda to gossip and leave the men for cigars and discussions on international politics, polo, golf, yachting and the next royal function. Later they come together for whist or the "American" game, and finally break up about midnight.

Around the table...half a dozen languages are heard...A tropical dinner, with the punkah swinging silently overhead, the men in white, the women in appropriate gowns, the table decorated with lotus flowers or heaped with white roses, the clean, lithe-limbed, white dressed, noiseless Chinese boys gliding about, the music of many languages, and the varied national types lending unique variety to the occasion, together with the mellowness and languor of the tropical air and the intermittent swish of oars in the waters of the neighbouring river, and the homely but cheerful call of the "*tokay*" [lizard] in the banyan tree is always remembered as quite delightful, even if your "no.1" boy comes and tells

you at the end of the third course, that the "No.1" cook has been suddenly seized with an attack of cholera!

The foreigners are too few to warrant a New York or London supply of delicacies, but we have served on our tables ice cream made in San Francisco and game purchased in the markets of London[.]

Nice Suit

Tailor and Cutter *magazine reporting on Chulalongkorn's European tour in 1897.*

It can be seen at a glance that his clothes were made by an English tailor. The King, judged by his dress, looks like a typical English gentleman. Perhaps the silk facing on the lapel of his neatly fitting coat is a little too heavy for the real West-End article, and, in one or two small matters of details, criticism might be justifiable; but taking the dress as a whole, it does credit to both his Majesty's good taste and to the tailor who produced the garment.

"The Durian is an excellent fruit, but offensive to some people's noses, for it smells very like human excrement, but when once tasted, the smell vanishes."
Scottish sea captain Alexander Hamilton, 1727

Has Your Stomach Been Filled Yet?

Hermann Norden in From Golden Gate to Golden Sun, *1923*

"Kin kao rue yang," said each newcomer [to the restaurant], and was greeted with the same words. I asked for an interpretation and got it: "Has your stomach been filled yet?" It seemed a strange phrase to be bandied about just before dinner, but I was told that it was the salutation of greeting at any hour of the day or night; that it merely took the place of our "How do you do?"

Chokechai Restaurant
In Peter Bennett's Flavours: Thailand's 200 Most Interesting Restaurants, *1972*

Snake? Bat's blood? Bear salad? Elephant knuckle? If such be your taste, Chokechai supplies the dishes. The game is fresh, much of it prepared at your table from just-killed animals. Mainly patronized by country people, the Chokechai is a bit difficult to find but the dining is al fresco, the dishes quite splendid, prices ridiculously low, and even if your taste doesn't run to crocodile tail, you'll be entranced by the atmosphere.

PS: Elephant knuckle must be ordered 48 hours ahead of time…defrosting, you know.

Snacks from the Skies
From Life and Ritual in Old Siam *by William J. Gedney, 1948*

People like to eat these waterbugs. It is very strange for they have an unpleasant odor…but people of every class, whether commoner or aristocrat, really like to eat them. They tear them apart and pound them up with pepper sauce or pickle them with fish sauce.

In Bangkok one sees people catching waterbugs at night. They are driven astray by rainstorms, and fly into big electric lights like those of the Plaza of the Equestrian Statue. Both children and adults watch to trap and catch them. When they fly low, people beat at them with cloths to knock them down.

Formerly the price for which they were sold was at the cheapest five satang. The upper classes in their automobiles also go to lie in wait, to trap and catch field waterbugs – or to buy them.

Mission Impossible

Siam's first Protestant missionaries were the colourful German Dr. Karl Gützlaff and the London Missionary Society's Rev. Jacob Tomlin, both of whom arrived in 1828. Ill health forced Tomlin back to Singapore after nine months, but Gützlaff stayed three years, during which he translated parts of the New Testament into Thai, authored a Siamese-English dictionary and learned the Fujian dialect spoken by some Chinese migrants. Neither Gützlaff nor Tomlin managed to convert a single Siamese.

The American Board of Commissioners for Foreign Missions sent their first emissaries in 1834, but had no more success. After 18 years without a convert, the organisation terminated its operation in Siam in 1849 and transferred its workers to China (where Gützlaff was by then something of a legend – dispensing bibles from opium ships).

The Catholic Church, whose first missionaries arrived in Thailand in the 1500s, had a local flock of 2,500 believers by 1830. The Siamese found it easier to appreciate Catholicism – at least its ritual aspects. While Protestant missionaries brought their wives with them and had children, Catholic priests, like Buddhist monks, were celibate, and used candles and incense in their worship. The priests' cassocks set them apart from ordinary men, and they built ornate churches – all of which resonated with the Siamese.

Rama IV had little time for Christianity. According to one account, he once (tongue in cheek, one suspects) challenged the Catholic fathers to convert 3,000 war prisoners.

No, Damn You!

In Christian Missions: Their agents, and Their Results by Thomas William M. Marshall, 1864

Captain Laplace also remarked during his stay in this country, that "the missionaries established in Siam are chiefly occupied in disputing with one another, and condemning each other to eternal fire."

"What you teach us to do is admirable, but what you teach us to believe is foolish."
King Mongkut to a Christian missionary

So Why Does He Let You Suffer?

From Journal of Nine Months' Residence in Siam by Jacob Tomlin, 1831

The Phra Klang [senior minister] had merely a cloth round his waist; is corpulent, and of a humorous turn, and was superintending a Dutch carpenter making some machine for him. During the whole of the conversation he held a common musket barrel in his hands. He put many questions to us, most of them trifling and ludicrous…Were our priests allowed to marry? On replying in the affirmative, he thought that was very good, but being restricted to one wife was rather hard.

Some of the Catholics whispered we were bad men – worse than heathen, believing neither in God, heaven, or hell! A bitter spirit was evidently working against us in the breasts of these Christians! – and we heard they had been previously much troubled at our coming hither…the Phra Klang, turning to the captain of the port, said, "If they (the Protestants) believe in the same God and Saviour Jesus Christ as the Catholics, why are you not all one?" The captain replied, "Protestants take wife!"

He then asked us what caused the cholera morbus…"If the God of heaven be the friend of Christians and not of idolaters, why did he afflict the Christians as well as the Siamese with cholera?" and, "Why not destroy the Siamese who worship other gods?"

Mr. H. replied, "They are spared till they hear his word, now sent to them by his servants."

A port in Bangkok, 1864

Amazing Doctor Dan

American Dr. Dan Beach Bradley – physician, writer, translator, printer, preacher and scholar – is one of the authentic heroes of modern Thai history. He came to Bangkok in July 1835 to preach the gospel, but found his medical skills in much greater demand. He was soon treating 100 patients a day, and introduced the Siamese to a variety of Western medical practices. Under the most primitive of conditions – often working outside before a crowd – he dared to try anything, even surgery. Among his more famous cases was a successful operation to remove a tumour – without anaesthesia – from the forehead of a Chinese man. Shortly after, he amputated the arm of a man injured by cannon misfire. The patient survived and became a monk. Dr. Bradley also concocted Siam's first successful smallpox vaccine from a scab embedded in a lump of beeswax he had brought with him from Boston.

In 1835, he imported the first printing press to Siam. His first publication was *The Ten Commandments*; followed by a proclamation for King Rama III, forbidding opium use. He also published the country's first newspaper and, in 1873, the first Thai dictionary.

As his reputation spread, he became physician and tutor to King Mongkut, appealing to the Buddhist monarch's intellectual curiosity about Western education and science. A man of strict and uncompromising morals, Bradley was known to leave parties if alcohol was served. He once published a critique describing the dinner parties hosted by Europeans as overindulgences in eating and drinking and "a host of consecutive evils." Dr Bradley's biggest disappointment in 39 years was that he managed to convert only one Siamese to Christianity. He died in Bangkok in 1873.

Pork-loving Christians

From The Eastern Seas by George Windsor Earl, 1837

Many native Christians are to be found at Bankok, probably about five or six hundred. These people are either descendants of the Portuguese who formerly traded on the coast, or converts to the Jesuits...They are despised both by the Europeans and the natives, and certainly not without cause: for they do no credit to any country which might own them. How the majority of these people contrive to live, it is impossible to say, but appearances are strongly against the supposition that they earn a subsistence by honest occupations.

Their communication with Europeans has enabled them to acquire a more extensive degree of knowledge than the natives, and some of them are consequently employed as interpreters and pilots, the captain of the port also belonging to this class. Their acquirements, however, are not always turned to a worthy use, and among other accomplishments of a very dubious nature, they are said to be complete adepts in pig-stealing, so much so, that a grunter can be whipped up and carried off without the least noise, and even without the animal itself being perfectly aware of the circumstance. Many a wretched Chinaman, who has been watching for weeks the gradual development of the sides and haunches of a fattening porker, awakes some morning, perhaps after dreaming of the feast he expects to enjoy in the course of a few days, and finds to his utter dismay that the pig has been abstracted from the sty during the night.

An Eye on the Clock

From Narrative of a Residence at the Capital of the Kingdom of Siam *by F.A. Neale, 1852*

Opposite the armoury, and just on the very threshold of his palace, was a very pretty little frame-house, surrounded with glass windows, and over the entrance-door to which was placed a board with the inscription of *"Watches and Clocks made and repaired here,"* written in large letters of gold…And here would [the crown prince] be seen, seated at a table that was liberally bestrewed with fragments and little mites of wheels, pursuing his favourite occupation of watchmaker.

It was a strange sight in such an out-of-the-way place as Bangkok, and amongst such a set of uncouth beings as the Siamese, to come suddenly upon the strange figure the Prince presented with a pair of huge goggles protruding from his eyes, and surrounded by a group of inquisitive and inquiring favourites. Watch-making and repairing were generally over about the time that the King's trumpet gave notice that he had had breakfast, and then the Prince retired to the harem, to partake of that pleasant meal also.

Royal Fathers

Kings of the Chakri Dynasty (1782-present) who produced the largest families:
1. King Mongkut (Rama IV): 82 children
2. King Chulalongkorn (Rama V): 77
3. King Buddha Loetla Nabhalai (Rama II): 73
4. King Jessadabodindra (Rama III): 51
5. King Buddha Yodfa Chulalok (Rama I): 42
Others: King Rama VI one child, Rama VIII and Rama VII no offspring. King Rama IX has four.

Healthy Delights

From King Maha Mongkut of Siam *by John Blofeld, 1972*

In one book, the King (Mongkut) is described as having been "bashful with the palace ladies." Whether this was really so seems doubtful. He was certainly no prude and undoubtedly took a healthy delight in the beauty of young girls. In one of his letters, he expressed undisguised envy of the Wang-Na (vice king), to whom princes and officials, encountered during his journeys up-country, used to offer their daughters in marriage.

King Mongkut complained that potential fathers-in-law kept well away from him and wondered why people regarded him as too old to welcome frequent offers of marriage, especially as the dashing Wang-Na was not so very much younger than himself.

Mae Nak

Bangkok's most famous ghost, Mae Nak, has reportedly been terrorising people for more than 150 years. During the reign of King Mongkut, Nak lived with her soldier husband in a house near a canal. While he was called away to war, the pregnant Nak died during childbirth. She became a ghost and when her unwitting husband returned she resumed living with him. When her unnatural behaviour – she stretched out her arm for three metres to pick up a dropped item – gave her away, he fled to a nearby temple. His actions provoked Nak to start spooking the neighbourhood. She agreed to stop her haunting spree when a monk promised that in her next life she would live again with her husband.

A shrine to Mae Nak was set up in Wat Mahabut and dozens of people visit her gold-leafed statue each day asking her spirit to bless them. Mae Nak's tale lives on in countless books, plays, musicals, movies and even a TV series.

Cute Kids

George B. Bacon, Siam, The Land of the White Elephant as It Is and Was, *1892*
Siamese children are the most fascinating little things. I was charmed with them from the very first moment, but it grieves me to think that some day they will become as ugly as their fathers and mothers – and that is saying much!

To the Editor

Siam's first newspaper, the Bangkok Recorder, *was a bi-weekly published in 1844 and '45 by American missionary Dr Dan Bradley, who also invented and cast Siamese type for printing. The* Bangkok Recorder *appeared in both English and Thai, had some 60 subscribers, who counted among its most avid readers – and frequent critics – King Mongkut. The Atlantic Monthly ran the following account of Anna Leonowens' experiences in the Siamese Court in 1870.*

His Majesty's mode of dealing with newspaper strictures (not always just) and suggestions (not always pertinent) aimed at his administration of public affairs, or the constitution and discipline of his household, was characteristic. He snubbed them with sententious arrogance, leavened with sarcasm.

His Majesty, however, enjoyed using the newspaper for occasional jibes, particularly at groups like missionaries, even the Pope himself. He wrote:
"The king of Siam, on reading from some European paper that the Pope had lately suffered the loss of some precious jewels, in consequence of a thief having got possession of his Holiness' keys, exclaimed, 'What a man! Professing to keep the keys of Heaven, and cannot even keep his own keys!'"

Later, the King – while doubtless pleased with his witty jibe at the Pope – apparently had second thoughts about upsetting the French missionaries in his community and retracted it in a later edition:
"What has been published in No. 25 of *Bangkok Recorder* thus: – The king, on perusal thereof denied that it is false. He knows nothing about his Holiness the Pope's sustaining loss of gems, & c., and has said nothing about religious faith."

But he still could not resist playing the role of Royal Proof-reader:
"Why name of [British Consul] Mr. Knox was not published thus: Missa Nok or Nawk?"

A Fatal Eclipse

King Mongkut was fascinated by Western science. After teaching himself astronomy, he built an observatory on the palace grounds, leading him to his greatest scientific triumph – and, indirectly, to his death.

In August 1868 the palace announced an expedition to view a solar eclipse. For villagers, eclipses were bad omens. Mongkut believed if he could predict the event with mathematical calculations, their superstition would evaporate. Invitations were sent to guests with the latitude and longitude of a spot on the Siamese coast where the king said the eclipse would be best observed. A mission of French astronomers journeyed from Paris to witness the event.

On August 18, 1868, at the exact second indicated by the king's calculations, the sky went totally dark. Mongkut and his prime minister cried "Hurrah! Hurrah!"

But the celebration was short-lived. In a matter of days, the king and several others in the royal party – including his 15-year-old son Chulalongkorn – fell ill with malaria contracted on the marshy, mosquito infested shore. Mongkut called his advisers to his bedside and, like the Buddha, died on his own birthday. He was 64 years old. Chulalongkorn recovered and succeeded to the throne as King Rama V.

Siamese City, Chinese Town

King Taksin (1768-1782), whose father was Chinese, encouraged Chinese immigration to revive the economy following Burma's destruction of Ayutthaya. All of Siam's monarchs until Rama VI followed suit. Chinese quickly found roles as middlemen, and were also skilled tradesmen and farmers who brought expertise in growing vegetables, pepper, sugar cane (Siam's first cash crop) and later rice.

By the mid-19th century Chinese comprised about half of Bangkok's population. The number continued to surge due to turmoil at home. Between 1882-1910 another million moved to Bangkok for work of which about 370,000 stayed. The Chinese weren't required to provide corvée labour to the king or bound by travel restrictions. In return they offered the government an energetic labour force, the spark of entrepreneurialism and a lucrative tax base. The first arrivals were mostly men, but Chinese women started arriving after 1910. More Chinese schools, business associations and newspapers followed, but this period also saw a rise in Thai nationalism. In 1913, the government passed the Nationality Act and the surname law, requiring all residents to take Thai family names. By 1925 it was estimated 95 percent of the city's industrial and commercial activity was in Chinese or Western hands. Subsequent programs excluded Chinese from

occupations like taxi driving, pig slaughtering, rice farming, selling petroleum, and labouring in fisheries and rubber plantations. The Chinese families were always agile enough to form alliances and maintain their dominant commercial position.

From the beginning, the centre of the Chinese community was Sampheng Lane, near the heart of today's Chinatown. At the turn of the century, the area was infamous for its vices – gambling, prostitution and opium – and a point of interest for almost all visitors. The two-story shop-houses that lined the street would become the standard Bangkok-style dwelling, spreading far into Siam's provincial cities.

Green Lanterns

The green lanterns of Sampheng's many brothels achieved nationwide notoriety, and the phrase "woman of Sampheng" became an epithet for a prostitute. Ernest Young describes the scene in The Kingdom of the Yellow Robe, 1898.

The one truly native quarter is a long narrow bazaar known as Sampeng. It is about a mile and a quarter in length, and contains a very mixed population of Indians, Siamese, and Chinese.

This long, narrow bazaar…is not without its own attractions. Here are gathered together specimens of all the native produce, and here too work a few exponents of each of the native crafts. Blacksmiths and weavers are plying their several trades; workers in gold and silver are fashioning boxes and ornaments for the rich, and the lapidaries are polishing stones for the jewellers to set.

Peep-shows and open-air theatres tempt the idle to linger, and numbers of busy toilers jostle each other as they make their way to and fro over the uneven, roughly paved foot-path. At night, the shops are closed, but the gambling-houses, opium-dens, and brothels are thronged by the lowest of the low.

A Chinese storefront selling seafood items

Melon Pip Gamble

From Rien que la Terre by *Paul Morand, 1925*

French author, playwright and poet Paul Morand was posted as a diplomat to Bangkok during the 1920s. The clamour of Yaowarat Road, Chinatown's main street, reduced even this elegant writer to exclamation marks.

With the noise of the street, the fanfare of gramophones, the clattering of mahjong, like hail on a tin roof, one is reminded of China, but it is the pawnshops which give the impression of reality. Gamblers come to pawn their jewels, their silken robes, their pipes. The more the pipes have been smoked and filled with opium, the more they gain for them. Lotteries, cockfights, fish fights, betting on Shanghai races, ten days' journey from here; all are played. Bets are even placed on the number of pips in a melon! It is reported that naval officers under arrest and confined to their boats, continue to play at sea, by signal!

"At Bang Luang on the small canal, many Chinese are selling pigs. Their wives are so young, fair, pretty, and rich it makes me feel shy and small. Thai men like me who asked for their hand would be blocked as if by iron bars. But if you have money like these Chinese, the bars just melt."

"Nirat Petch", *Thai poet Sunthorn Phu (1786-1855)*

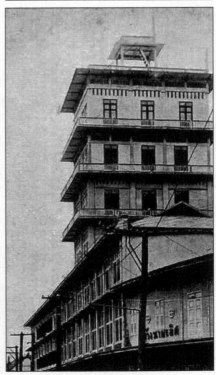

Nai Lert Building

This Is Chinese Bangkok

H. *Warington Smyth*, Five Years in Siam, 1898

My business, however, soon took me to the other Bangkok that we are yet to mention. A long drive along an unutterably filthy road, where thrive the most unsurpassed of smells, to which dead dogs, diseased Chinamen, or festering drains all give their contribution; where Chinese cook stalls, and rickety gharries; where those receivers of stolen goods called pawn-shops offer valuable watches, curios, or pistols for a song; and where such gentlemen as HANG ON, dentist, and SAW LONG, carpenter, display their boards. This is Chinese Bangkok, malodorous and ill-mannered.

The Postman Cometh

From *The Kingdom of the Yellow Robe* by Ernest Young, 1898

The absence of surnames, and also of numbered houses in most of the streets, causes some difficulty when it becomes necessary to send letters through the post. An envelope has often to be addressed something like the following:

To MR. LEK,
Student of the Normal College
Son of Mr. Yai, Soldier,
Near the foot of the Black Bridge
at the back of the Lotus Temple
New Road, Bangkok.

"[The Chinese] shout a lot and work; the Siamese, gentler, pass by silently."
Charles Buls, Siamese Sketches, *1901*

Revolt of the Triads

Secret societies had great influence in the early Chinese community, and for the most part the government was happy to entrust them with keeping the order. But occasionally the gangs ran riot, as happened June 1889, when the Tang Kong Xi (Teochiu) and Siew Li Kue (Fujian) triads fought a pitched three-day battle on the New Road, near the main European enclave. An estimated 20 people were killed and 150 wounded. After the violence ended, the troops sent in to quell the fighting (including some Danish marines) tied Chinese prisoners together by their pigtails in groups of one hundred as humiliation. The aftermath was reported in the Bangkok Times *on 20 July 1889.*

The enquiry into the cases of the Chinese rioters who have been captured and sentences passed and confirmed by H.M. the King. Out of the Ang Yee society ringleaders, including the woman Ma Lao, eight are sentenced to receive 60 lashes each and to be imprisoned with harsh labour for terms of 7, 5 and 3 years respectively. The flogging part of the sentence was carried into effect in public, near the Central Gaol. Eight ringleaders, wearing neck chains in addition to ankle chains, then received 60 strokes each, some of them with great stoicism. The punishment concluded, the prisoners were conducted back to Gaol.

King Chulalongkorn

Rama IV tried to shift Bangkok's foreign policy priorities from China to the West, but his reign was ultimately one of transition. Delivering Siam into the new world order fell to his son, Chulalongkorn (1853-1910).

In Thailand, Rama V is best remembered as the monarch who introduced modernity while keeping the colonial powers – most noticeably France – at bay, thereby preserving the country's independence and pride. But the internal pressures on him were no less strong. To reduce the clout of nobles in Bangkok and more distant regions, Chulalongkorn centralised power in the hands of the royal family and extended the capital's influence via new waterways, roads, railroads and, most importantly, laws.

Chulalongkorn introduced reforms to revolutionize the social hierarchy, ending slavery and eroding the power of local chiefs over labour pools. He overhauled the army and police force, started on nationwide public works and spread elementary public education to the most distant provinces. By the end of Chulalongkorn's reign, Bangkok was no longer the seat of a sacred kingdom ruled by an unseen king. It was the administrative centre of a modern nation state.

The Rightful Heir

From King Maha Mongkut of Siam *by John Blofeld, 1972*

[Mongkut] ordered the ministers to select one of his brothers or nephews [as successor]. He forbade them to choose Prince Chulalongkorn, although this astute and able young man was his eldest son by a full queen; he pointed out that the boy, not yet recovered from his illness, was only fifteen years old and therefore too young and inexperienced to tackle the immense task of saving Siam from annexation and carrying out the great programme of reform he had initiated. Furthermore, were the choice to fall on him, his life would be

endangered as the more conservative princes and nobles would be bitterly disappointed.

On 30 September [1868], the day before the King's death, Chaophraya Suriyawongsa pointed out that the Western powers took it for granted that the eldest son (by a queen) would succeed. Were someone else chosen, they might regard (or pretend to regard) him as a usurper and withhold recognition. Though the minister did not say so, the implication was that Britain or France might invade the country to 'restore the rightful heir' and, having done so, remain there, first as protector and later as suzerain. Reluctantly the King agreed and, in the evening, sent his son two gifts – a ring and a gold rosary, which had once belonged to the founder of the dynasty – as symbols of his forthcoming elevation. Very wisely, the minister had the young prince's guard doubled.

"The Siamese people, gentle and intelligent, will they protect themselves…with a new courage against their native sluggishness? Or will these foreign germs be murderous for them, like those that ferment in the swamps of the Menam?"
Former Brussels mayor Charles Buls, 1901

Battle of the Chao Phraya

In July 1893, after a string of skirmishes involving its troops in disputed areas of Siamese-controlled Indochina, France ordered two gunboats up the Chao Phraya River towards Bangkok. The state-of-the-art vessels, *Inconstante* and *Comète*, quickly laid waste to the Chula Chom Klao Fort at the mouth of the river and its almost medieval battery of muzzle cannons. At that time at least 25 Danish naval officers were serving with the Siamese Navy. Copenhagen had forbidden them to fight the French, but they nevertheless did. Walter Christmas, a Danish captain in charge at the fort, fired his cannon four times. When he tried a fifth time, it collapsed. The battle lasted less than an hour.

The gunboats anchored off the French Embassy, menacingly close to the Royal Palace. After a short standoff, Siam conceded to France large parts of Indochina, which it had claimed rights or suzerainty.

Demoralised

From the diary of Gustave Rolin-Jaequemyns, Belgian adviser to King Chulalongkorn, 1893

Everybody seems to be demoralized. The King asks me what I think will happen and de Richelieu [Danish commander of the Siamese navy] proposes to try to launch two Siamese ships against the two French, to sink them. I ask if there are serious chances that the operation will be successful. He can barely bring himself to say so. This being the case, I emphatically advise against an operation which I would even hesitate to recommend if success would be anticipated. Inevitably this would mean war in case of success and in case of failure it would mean the bombardment of Bangkok and of the Palace. My reply is that we must, in the interest of the city, abstain from hostilities.

Fighting the Ennui

Despite France's interest in Siam, very few French lived in Bangkok at the end of the 19th century. Some reports (mostly British) said the French weren't very popular in the city. According to Lucian Fournereau, in Bangkok in 1892 *(1894), the feeling was mutual.*

Distractions, no! Nothing here is the equivalent of what they have in Saigon, la rue Catinat, and so French. No cafes, no theatres, no concerts, no...gypsies; no European quarter, no visits. Mon Dieu – it is boring!

What remains therefore to make the Oriental life tolerable? Nothing. Bangkok has two clubs: one English, the other German, with little entertainment. Life at home...married men with their wives, celibate with their boredom. Vae Solis!

"It was a hodgepodge of hopeless ships, useless guns and incompetent crews, commanded by men who, however stout and resourceful in other fields, for the most part were without knowledge in military skills."
Captain Walter Christmas, 1890s

"The French colonists mix more with the natives than do the British; they are not so distant as the latter, but being by turns familiar and angry, they do not make themselves respected by their servants."
Emile Jottrand, 1905

LA FRANCE AU SIAM

In 1861 the European diplomats and residents in Bangkok petitioned Rama IV to build a new road so they could "enjoy horseback riding for physical fitness and pleasure". The government agreed, and established Charoen Krung Road, better known among the foreign community as New Road, along the river.

"One of the most annoying and grievous circumstances of any business in this country, is the delay incident in travelling even from one part of Bangkok to the other. When a person wishes to transact any business a mile distant which, at home, would easily be done in an hour, it will ordinarily require three or four."

Rev. John Taylor Jones, 1836

The No. 1 Tram

From In the Lands of the Sun: Notes and Memories of a Tour in the East *by Prince Wilhelm of Sweden, 1915*

A few years ago only horse-trams were to be found, and it is related that when electricity first took its place among the means of transport of modern Bangkok, the natives fell on their knees and worshipped the wheels of the cars, convinced that they must be the abode of good spirits. Nor did any one venture to take a ride in them, and it was only when the old King had shown his subjects a good example that the traffic was resumed…The tram-cars offer certain advantages to strangers, since at any rate they are compelled to follow the lines laid down for them, and cannot, like the rickshaws, turn and twist with him through the most impossible streets, from the maze of which it may be difficult to find a way out.

For as a rule a coolie speaks no other language than his own, and if you give him an address and ask if he understands English, he unfailingly answers with a broad grin.

Where the Classes Meet

From A Woman of Bangkok *by Jack Reynolds, 1956*

The street was choked with the usual traffic; overloaded, lop-sided buses with battered tinwork and radiators pouring steam and water; wooden-wheeled rickshaws tugged by Chinese men in wheel-like hats, their black shirts plastered to their sweating shoulders and their black pants rolled up on their knotted thighs; sleek luxurious private cars transporting the rich from homes that lacked nothing the heart could desire to resorts where they could throw away their inexhaustible wealth; samlors with strident bells, bicycles, trams, motor-scooters, everything except bullock carts, it seemed.

Gridlock Capital

In Carol Hollinger's Mai Pen Rai Means Never Mind, *1965*

My first afternoon in Bangkok I set out at 3pm to surprise a friend who had warned I would not be seeing much of him. The first hundred yards took fifteen minutes. A half hour later I had travelled a mile. There was no accident or breakdown; just too many vehicles trying to cross two busy intersections. The air-conditioner seized up and we rolled down the windows. The pollution set my eyes itching. Other drivers read, dozed or stared glassy-eyed. My driver muttered to himself, manicured his fingernails, and handed me tissues for wiping my face. At five minute intervals he slapped his forehead and then turned to flash a beatific, apologetic smile...It was 95 degrees and humid, and in 10 minutes I had sweated through my clothes. A terrified family of tourists gripped one another like a string of paper dolls as they inched across a murderous intersection. Later, a Thai asked me, "Do you know what we call a person who crosses a Bangkok street safely? We call him the 'winner'!"

A Guide to Taking Taxis in Bangkok

Adele Chidakel in The New York Times, *Apr. 28, 1963*

The streets swarm with cars from every country with an assembly plant. The little Japanese models are especially popular, and occasionally, one even sees an American car. It looks like a beetle that blundered into an ants' nest.

As a result, the sensible mode of transportation is by taxi. All the cabs are tiny – two in the back is snug – and all have efficient-looking meters. But nobody ever uses the meters. It costs more that way, the Thais explain.

The easy way to travel by cab is to have a Thai friend hail a taxi and tell the driver to take you to your destination, wait for you, and bring you back. The friend also negotiates the total price. But that is the coward's way.

The adventurous do-it-yourself way requires that you have the address written in Thai.

You hail a cab, point to the address and either make an offer or wait for the driver to set a price. Then you bargain. Numbers are indicated by Thai, English or fingers...The driver will probably reply by pointing out, with suitable gestures that he has a wife, four children and sick mother to support, and that could not even buy gas alone at that price. Then he will make a counter offer... For this stage of the negotiations, one should memorize one key Thai phrase – *mark kern pai*. This means, "That's too much," and should be uttered in a tone of shocked disbelief with accompanying facial expression and perhaps a half-step away from the taxi.

The formalities over, you can get down to business...This is important. When the driver asks the same sum twice, he is very close to the proper price. If you offer 1 baht under that, he will probably accept it, and you have yourself a fair bargain.

GETTING AROUND

TRICYCLE TAXIS (known as samlor to the Bangkokian) are Bangkok's most typical form of transport. But it is also a leisurely one, so take a taxi when you are in a hurry. A samlor drive in the cool of the evening is a most pleasant experience and one you should not miss. As there are no fixed rates, it is best to agree upon a price with the driver before you set out, if you are going to a definite destination. For a trip of ten minutes Tcs. 5.—; half an hour Tcs. 15.—

BUSSES AND TRAMS operate on nearly all the main streets. As they are Bangkok's cheapest form of transport they are generally fairly crowded and consequently rather warm. Apart from this, since trams run on single lines, these are rather slow. Busses, on the _____ generally drive as fast as they can and only need a few

"Though supposedly 'smiling' and 'passive' in ordinary life, the Thai behind the wheel of a small Japanese taxi shows kamikaze tendencies. His speciality is to stamp on the accelerators at the sight of a red light or a jaywalker, then brake at the last split second. He grins wonders at the barbarian who complains."

Peter Braestrup, 1966

Life in the Slow Lane

Maxine North, who came to Thailand in 1950 as the wife of an undercover CIA agent and went on to found Thailand's largest bottled-water company, Polaris, in the LA Times *(1972).*

The city wasn't designed for cars. When we arrived there were hardly any cars, but there was traffic. The streets were so narrow – you had a *klong* on either side – that you couldn't even pass. Most people traveled by *samlor*.

The Oriental

In 1881, Hans Niels Andersen, a young Danish businessman with interests in Bangkok that grew into the East Asiatic Company, bought a small hotel on the riverbank called The Oriental. He hired an Italian architect to oversee its redesign and opened the property in 1887 with "forty commodious and well furnished bedrooms." The new Oriental offered features never seen in Siam outside of a royal palace: a second floor (in a time of single-story bungalows), carpeted hallways, smoking and ladies' rooms, a billiard room and a bar seating 50 – with a barman named "Spider" – and a French chef lured away from the consulate. The Oriental, with its vibrant river setting, came to symbolise Bangkok as a destination of indulgent, exotic, lavish elegance. Attracted by its mystique, a throng of writers have checked in to the Authors' Wing over the years including: Victor Hugo, Fyodor Dostoyevsky, Henrik Ibsen, Leo Tolstoy, Emile Zola, Thomas Hardy, Henry James, Robert Louis Stevenson, Oscar Wilde, George Bernard Shaw, Joseph Conrad, Arthur Conan Doyle, Rudyard Kipling, Maxim Gorky, Somerset Maugham, Ernest Hemingway, Noel Coward, Barbara Cartland, Georges Simenon, George Orwell, Evelyn Waugh and James Michener.

Telegrams:
ORIENHOTEL, BANGKOK

Oriental Hotel ✠

Bangkok

Oldest and most Popular Hotel in all of Siam. Situated on river front, fine gardens, French Chef. Cuisine and all appointments first class—rates moderate. Our Steam Launch meets all Steamers, also Auto Car at disposal of guests. *Now being remodeled.* Modern Toilet Fittings, Etc. ALL LANGUAGES SPOKEN

Proprietor: A. Maire

Dead Guests Not Welcome

Somerset Maugham describes a bout of malaria he had at The Oriental in The Gentleman in the Parlour *(1930), written at the hotel while he was recuperating.*

It was apparently a bad attack, since for some days the quinine had no effect on me; my temperature soared to those vertiginous heights that are common in malaria, and neither wet sheets nor ice packs brought it down. I lay there panting and sleepless, and shapes of monstrous pagodas and great gilded Buddhas bore down on me. Those wooden rooms with their verandahs made every sound frightfully audible to my tortured ears, and one morning I heard the manageress of the hotel – Mme Marie – an amiable creature but a good woman of business, in her guttural German voice say: "I can't have him die here, you know, you must take him to the hospital."

And the doctor replied: "All right. But we'll wait a day or two yet."

"Well, don't leave it too long," she replied.

Rooms to Spare

From The 1904 Traveller's Guide to Bangkok and Siam *by J. Antonio*

Bangkok is veritably a city of Hotels, that is to judge by the number of sign boards which meet the eye everywhere, but few of these can be recommended. The leading one is the Oriental where extensive improvements and additions have of late been made. The stranger may also be made comfortable at the Hotel de la Paix (better known to Bangkokians as Mme Toni's), the Hotel d'Europe, or the Bristol or Palace Hotels.

Pomp, Pageantry and Problems

King Vajiravudh's coronation in 1911 was a spectacular affair, attracting members of the British, Russian and Japanese royal families, heads of state and other foreign dignitaries. The festivities lasted for 13 days and consumed a staggering eight percent of the national budget. It would come to signal not only the beginning of Rama VI's reign, but also the start of a protracted fight on how the national treasury – and overall government – should be administered. The British-educated Vajiravudh was by official accounts a "literary genius" who produced an endless stream of plays, essays and other writings. He was less skilled as a national leader. Over his 15-year reign, the royal family's grip on power, which had never been stronger than under Chulalongkorn, weakened and the national coffers ran dry. By 1925, the end of Vajiravudh's reign, the country was in economic distress and political turmoil soon followed.

Civilised Water

Siamese, who had long distilled their own version of rice whiskey, got their first taste of beer and Western whiskey in the reign of Rama V. Beer was at first called *nam sivilai*, or civilised water (*sivilai* was applied to a number of items and ideas and was intended to reflect Siam's development). In the 1920s, aristocrat Phya Bhirom Bhakdi established the country's first brewery, which produced Singha Beer from Thai hops and German barley. Singha, like most Thai beers that followed, had a high level of alcohol so that it could be drunk with ice without losing its punch.

Gala Performance

Prince Wilhelm of Sweden, describing Vajiravudh's coronation, in In the Lands of the Sun, *1915*

The Siamese did not wish to be behind their European models...Thus it was that "Gala Performance" appeared on the programme – make your arrangements accordingly!

And a performance it was, which in duration easily beat all precedents among us Occidentals. For it began at 9 p.m. and was not over before half-past two in the morning. Now, good reader, you must not suppose that this was an absolutely unmixed delight, however much you might perhaps have enjoyed the splendid costumes or the brilliant house. For to sit five hours on end – with only *one* short *entr'acte* – when the thermometer is at about 105° and the mosquitoes are unmercifully supping on your ankles, certainly has its drawbacks. But in spite of this, the evening – though somewhat long – was nevertheless extraordinarily interesting...Every time an actor enters, he begins by kneeling to the King and showing his deference by striking his forehead three times against the stage. Then only does he take up his part.

Englishmen in Their Exile

John Anderson, M.D., from the documents of the British East India Company, 1620

Gambling was not the only foible of those days as was amply proved by references to lewdness, nameless diseases, drunkenness, and bastard children now and again cropping up in the correspondence of the Company's servants. Morality may have had a lower standard in those days than it has now, but these Englishmen in their Exile, their surroundings so different from those encompassing their lives in an English home, and the novel temptations to which they were exposed, lead charity to be merciful in judging them.

Thailand's colourful foreign influence is reflected best in the uniforms of her armed services. British advisers to the Siamese royal court contributed to the splendorous formal dress uniforms worn by high-ranking officers and guards of honour for ceremonial occasions, which date back to the reign of King Chulalongkorn. Many of the distinctive service uniforms for lower ranks were patterned on those of the United States, while for years enlisted navy personnel wore uniforms resembling their French counterparts.

By Jove, If We Controlled Siam

From Brown Women and White *by Andrew Freeman, 1932*

"When this road was first built the trains didn't run at night because of collisions with elephants."

"You're kidding me," I said.

The Englishman poured another drink.

"No really," he said. "There ought to be a law requiring all stray elephants to have head and tail lights."

"By jove, if we controlled Siam, we'd put the country on an efficient basis. These people are not fit to govern themselves."

"Why not?" I asked.

"Well look around you. Look how they do things. The Oriental will never appreciate what the white man has done for him, that's why. If we handled our affairs like the Siamese do, where would we be?"

"Half of the European residents are English. In fact, to the casual observer Bangkok appears as much English as Aden [in British Yemen]."

Capt. G.J. Younghusband, 1888

Caste Distinctions
From Chequered Leaves *by Eric Read, 1913*

"The people are very nice, but it takes you some time to know the colony of course."

"Of course," rashly affirmed Juggins, feeling he was on terra firma at last, but alas, it was terracotta.

"The caste distinctions are very strict there, and then you know the life they lead! But we will draw a veil over that. It is a species of knowledge that had better dawn gently upon you. Still, if you are fond of conviviality, I may say there is the bridge clique, and the horsey clique, and the musical clique, and the stengah clique to choose from."

"Stengah?"

"Well, stengah is Malay for a half, so I fancy the stengah clique could be described as the 'half-measures society,' only they don't seem to live up to the half-measures standard, in the figurative or liquid sense, so to say. If you become a member of the Bangkok 'Benighted Club', you will hear all about it, and learn to distinguish. The history and development of these cliques form an interesting study."

Judge, Jury and Executioner

In 1896 W. A. R. Wood was posted to Bangkok at age 18. Starting as a student interpreter, he was the youngest consular officer ever to go to Thailand – probably to any Eastern post. In Consul in Paradise: Sixty-eight years in Siam, 1965, *he writes*:

It is not a very pleasant job, hanging a man, but it was all part of the day's work for a British Consul in Siam when I was young.

Domestic Bliss

John Barrett, ex-Minister Resident and US Consul General to Bangkok, in The New York Times, July 4, 1901

Servants are not a problem in Asia – they are a pleasure. In Bangkok, the house servants of foreigners are usually Chinese. The average household has a "No 1" or head boy who acts as butler, valet, headwaiter and general supervisor or majordomo. He is assisted by the "No.2" boy who does any of the heavier work that does not become the "No.1". These two are assisted by the "No 3" boy who might however also be called the "No.1" coolie. This coolie may either be a man, who has long done coolie labour, or a "learn pidgin" boy, i.e. one who while acting as coolie, aspires some day to become a full fledged "boy". This term "boy" is applied to household servants generally in the Orient and has no reference to age, size or experience. Many a "boy" has passed the age of 60 and still remained a faithful servant. Occasionally, if a master wishes to show special favour he does not call his servant "boy" but salutes him as "Chin", "Teng", "Lek", or whatever may be his name.

In the kitchen we again find the numeral arrangement of cooks – two of them, and one coolie for the heavy work. Then comes the stable. Here there is a change of nationality. The man who looks after the horses is a Malay – sometimes a Siamese – who has one or more numbered assistants, according to the number of horses.

Next we note the laundry. Here we have either a Chinaman or a native Siamese woman. If you are a bachelor, you have the former, for fear the neighbours may talk. The washman is called the "dobe."

Finally we have the men who look after the grounds or "compound". In Bangkok they are commonly referred to as boatmen because, aside from cleaning the lawn and filling the bathroom tank, they "chow" or propel the boat which everyone possesses in order to go about on the wide river and numerous canals. Three of these at least are required. They are always Siamese and rank also by numbers.

I must not leave out the watchman – the noble Indian – the "Sikh" who is supposed to guard the premises by night and never sleep, but is always found sleeping!

Norbury
Bangkok

The Good Life

From Life, *Dec. 31, 1951*

Unlike other parts of Asia, where Americans and other Westerners now have to step carefully, the changes in the Thai government had absolutely no effect on the foreigners in Bangkok. Because Thailand, an independent monarchy for six centuries, was never anybody's colony, there is no resentment against "foreign imperialists." When one American family got caught in the middle of a political upset last June and had to flee its home, it returned to find nothing missing or damaged except a zinnia patch, which had been blown up by a stray mortar shell. The 300 Americans living there, mostly employees of the U.S. government and the big concession companies, mingle freely and easily with Thais of all classes and even marry them without fear of being ostracized by other Westerners. All in all, Westerners find Bangkok one of the finest places in the world to live.

Train Tipplers

In Bangkok Daily Mail, *1915*

There is no doubt whatever that on occasions like this [festival at Paknam temple] the consumption of strong liquors is greatly on the increase. Ten years ago or less it was not considered proper; now it is a common sight.

On the train from Bangkok it was not at all uncommon to see people solacing themselves against the rigors of an hour journey by pulls from a bottle of beer and not over-clean conversation; whilst pilgrims of a decade ago were content with betel and lime and discussing the prospects of a crop.

Americans Abroad

Henry Cook in a letter to The Times, *Dec. 8, 1958*

Your dispatch of Nov. 23 "Bangkok Hobby: Temple Rubbing" describing the activities of American women, among others, in the Buddhist temple, is more timely than you may realize. Many are reading a novel called "The Ugly American."

How long would we tolerate similar action in some of our Fifth Avenue churches – or even on commercial buildings? People who cannot represent us abroad with at least the basic dignity that demands respect for the host's institutions would be better left at home. Their actions belittle all of us in the eyes of the country's nationals and undermined the commanding statues we want our diplomats to have abroad.

Part of the statement made by the Italian secretary's wife describes the situation accurately. "It is really dirt cheap..."

Betel Mania

Betel boxes in the Ayutthaya period had symbolised the noble office with their distinguished and lavish design. Nobles would proceed through the streets proudly displaying their betel boxes. In 1943, despite widespread protest – including from his own mother – Phibul banned chewing betel nut. A European visitor in the 1930s explains the reasons behind the ban:

The floor [of Bangkok's largest cinema – the "Phathanakorn"] is filthy; indeed it is absolutely disgusting. Some people squirt betel juice all over the place; it bounces off the ground and sprays all over the clothing of other patrons. Should you go to the movies barefoot and tread in this goo you'll be doubly revolted.

Chariots of the Gods

Sao Ching Cha – the Giant Swing – is among Bangkok's most unusual landmarks. It was first built in the 18th century for use in a Brahmin ceremony that re-enacted Shiva's descent into the world. The tricky part of the ceremony involved the human "naga serpents" who rode the swing high above Bangkok's skyline as they attempted to retrieve bags of silver coins with their teeth. The ceremony was abolished in 1935 following a string of deaths involving the participants – but the towering wooden structure has been preserved.

Imitation Hokum

From Geoffrey Gorer's Bali and Angkor, *1936*

Thai architecture is the same as Cambodian, but with knobs on – lots of knobs. Bangkok is the most hokum place I have ever seen, never having been to California. It is a triumph of the "imitation" school; nothing is what it looks like; if it is not parodying European buildings it is parodying Khmer ones; failing anything else it will parody itself.

Raising the Tricolour

For decades Siam's flag featured a white elephant on a red background. However, many foreigners apparently couldn't recognise the animal, especially when the flag was flapping. In 1916 King Vajiravudh looked out his window and was mortified to see a flag hanging upside down, the international signal of distress. He decided a new design was needed. Out went the white elephant and a new flag was created with a blue central stripe to reflect the King's birthday color, white for Buddhism and red for the blood that Thai people should be prepared to shed for the country. The red, white and blue flag was also similar to the national flags of many of the Allies whom Siam was supporting in World War I. The king declared the new flag should be known as the *Trairanga*, the five-stripe national flag of Siam – instantly recognisable no matter how it was hung.

Late to the Party

In From Golden Gate to Golden Sun *by Hermann Norden, 1923*

We drove back to the green space in the city, where stands the white shaft erected in memory of the Siamese who fell in the World War. Some, with humorous intent declare that the monument is literally to *the* Siamese who fell; that there was only one of him. Be that as it may, Siam certainly equipped regiments of little yellow-skinned soldiers who marched away in June, 1918, to bear a hand in the terrible struggle. And every man of them who returned came back limping. European shoes can be as crippling as European bullets to feet that have always been free and bare.

117

Siam's Mystery Speedster

On the motor racing tracks of Europe, the pseudonym "B Bira" hid the identity of Prince Birabongse Bhanubandh, grandson of Rama IV – a star of European Formula One now remembered for his skilful and charismatic driving.

The young Prince Bira was sent in 1927 to Eton College and later to study at Cambridge. His cousin, Prince Chula Chakrabongse, encouraged the 21-year-old Bira to try his hand at motor racing. In Bira's first race in Ireland in 1936 he finished second. The success prompted him to become a Formula One and Grand Prix driver, racing for the Maserati, Gordini and Connaught teams, among others.

During World War II he trained as a glider pilot and set several British records. In 1954, Bira won the Grand Prix des Frontières on the Chimay road circuit and the New Zealand Grand Prix before announcing his retirement from racing. He took up sailing, competing in the Olympic Games in Melbourne, Rome and Munich. Bira – a restless soul – went on to run an airline, marry three times, and become a skilled sculptor whose work was exhibited at the Royal Academy.

อากคยท ๑๐ ธันวาคม ๒๔๘๒

BANGKOK GRAND PRIX
INTERNATIONAL MOTOR RACE
SUNDAY, DECEMBER 10, 1939

Left: *Prince Birabongse Bhanutej Bhanubandh of Siam (B.Bira) at the wheel of a Maserati for the 1951 grand prix season.*
Right: *A Bira poster, 1947. The prince was the only royal to ever compete in Formula One.*

The Last Buffalo

Prince Wilhelm of Sweden was one of the guests at Vajiravudh's grand coronation. In between official functions, he managed to get in a spot of hunting rare animals, as related in In the Lands of the Sun: Notes and Memories of a Tour in the East *(1915).*

The next day – the last of the year – we arrived safely at Bangkok, tired, but with nothing but pleasant memories of an interesting shooting expedition. And the buffalo horns from Ban Chee-wan are at present the proudest specimen among my hunting trophies, since, as far as I know, Lewenhaupt and I are the only Europeans who have ever shot any of this species of the Siamese fauna. And in future it will be still harder – not to say impossible – to bring down these animals, as on account of the small number of them in the country it is proposed to protect them altogether.

Young Revolutionaries

By the time Thai law student Pridi Panomyong and his young military allies staged their revolution in June 1932, the country was ready for change. The 1929 collapse of Wall Street had caused turmoil in faraway Siam. Farmers' incomes fell by half as rice prices plummeted. City workers and bureaucrats had their salaries cut. The royal government responded to shortfalls in its reserves by hiking taxes, causing further disenchantment with the ruling elite. Whereas Pridi's vision for the country was based on the liberal socialism he'd discovered in France – as had contemporaries Deng Xiaoping, Zhou Enlai, Ho Chi Minh and, a little later, Saloth Sar (aka Pol Pot) – his uniformed allies saw the nationalist model – espoused by Japan's militaristic government and Italian dictator Benito Mussolini – as the key to Siam's future. Over the next 17 years, Pridi was in and out of government, but his legacy was considerable. He wrote the country's first democratic constitution, which included grassroots-level elections, started nationalising much of Thailand's industry, created the central bank and a prestigious university, headed the anti-Japanese resistance during World War II and served as regent to young Rama VIII. Once Pridi was banished after being branded a communist by his rightest rivals, fleeing first to China and then France, Thailand's generals were free to fight over the spoils of power. And they did for the next 50 years.

"In accordance with the Fifth Edict, the government would like all Thai people to consume noodles because the noodle is a good food containing all things, rice, nuts and sour, salty, and sweet flavors, which all are produced in Thailand. The noodle is nutritious, clean, cheap, easy to buy, and tastes good."

Government radio broadcast, Nov. 7, 1939

Out with the Old, In with the New

To accelerate Siam's "progress", Field Marshal Plaek Phibulsongkram (better known as Phibul), who came to power in 1938, issued a series of cultural mandates to ensure the kingdom would be recognised by foreigners as a "civilised and modernised country". The edicts included what to eat and wear and how to behave. Phibul also changed the name of the country from Siam to Thailand, insisted central Thai be spoken in the place of regional dialects, and ordered people to hang photos of him in their homes, while banning those of King Prajadhipok, who had abdicated. Phibul was the first military general to take the rank of field marshal, which had previously been reserved for the king. As for the people of Thailand, he asked that they refer to him simply as "the Leader".

Phibul's government also ruled that noodle manufacturing was an occupation reserved for Thais. Before the official push, noodles weren't widely eaten outside of Bangkok's Chinese neighbourhoods. Not long after, Phibul's wife, La-iad, claimed credit for inventing *phat Thai*, based on a Vietnamese dish.

> "Phibul forbade Siamese to go without hats or shoes, to chew betel nut, to sit on the streets, or to wear the panung (native skirt). In official photographs, shoes and hats were painted on unshod, hatless peasants. Phibul ordered officials to kiss their wives when they left for their Government offices. Violators of his decrees were whisked off to 'self-improvement centers.' "
>
> Time, *Nov. 24, 1947*

Sawatdee

For many visitors, the most endearing custom of Thais is their greeting known as the wai – slight bow with palms pressed together in prayer-like fashion usually accompanied with the salutation "*sawatdee*". Up until the 1930s, the usual greeting on the streets of Bangkok was the far more prosaic "*pai nai*" (Where are you going?) or "*kin khao yang*" (Have you eaten rice yet?).

Sawatdee was coined in the mid-1930s by Phraya Upakit Silapasan of Chulalongkorn University. The word was derived from the Sanskrit *svasti*, which had previously been used in Thai only as a formulaic opening to inscriptions. *Sawatdee*, incidentally, has the same Sanskrit root as *swastika* which, ironic as it may sound to Westerners, translates literally to "that which is associated with well-being".

121

Bangkok's "Monument to Democracy" – designed by Corrado Feroci, an Italian trained in the monumental classicism favoured by Mussolini – celebrates the end of absolute monarchy in Thailand in 1932. It was built in 1939 at the order of Field Marshal Phibul. Since 1932, there has been a military intervention in government, on average, every three and a half years. The monument was only two years old at the time of the first coup.

122

When Japanese troops invaded Indochina in 1940, Phibul sent troops across the border to seize parts of French Cambodia. The armed clashes with the French were inconclusive, and the Japanese, irritated by the fighting between its allies, ordered a halt to hostilities. Phibul nevertheless declared victory and ordered work on Bangkok's Victory Monument. The 600 names on the monument are all of Thai soldiers killed during World War II.

Gathering Storm

Radio Bangkok, Nov. 11, 1941
The entry of Thailand into the war is only a matter of time...The Thai government has in the past tried to lull your anxiety by saying the world situation is improving, but now we realize that it is better to be frank. So to all Thais we say – Get ready for war. Learn how to fight under competent authorities[.]

[Secret]
From Canton To: Tokyo
December 2, 1941
J-19
#512 Secret outside the department
If hostilities are to begin we here are all prepared. The army has completed all preparations to move immediately upon Thailand. Should the British resist to the bitter end, it is understood that the army is prepared to go so far as to militarily occupy the country.
(Japanese) Army 26103
Japanese diplomatic message intercepted by US intelligence in 1941

Pressured into War

A passage from Nicol Smith's Into Siam: Underground Kingdom, *1945, in which the Thai foreign minister of the time, Direk Jayanam, describes the circumstances leading up to Thailand's military alliance with Japan.*

"[Ambassador Yamamoto] wanted me to authorize free passage of Japanese troops across Siam. I protested that we were neutral, but he said that for Japan it was a matter of life or death. The military attache, General Tamura, said delay meant bloodshed...and announced that 'At this moment Japanese troops are landing at various places in Siam!' "

"Prime Minister Field Marshal Pibul arrived and called a cabinet meeting.

"The neutral members were quickly put down.

"Pibul then asked the opinion of the Minister for Defence, an opportunist who could be counted upon to follow the premier. He agreed that we couldn't stand up against the Japs.

"Having received the answer he wanted, Pibul...declared it was obvious it would be futile to attempt to stop the Japanese and said he would order our soldiers to cease firing."

War Years

While officially an ally, Japan treated Thailand like an occupied country, stationing 50,000 troops on Thai territory throughout the war and plundering the economy to supply its army in Burma. Thais were called upon to provide food, supplies and labour to Japanese camps. The war was disruptive to the capital, where essentials were in short supply, and almost all goods had to be recycled. Ash from fires was turned into soap, mosquito nets into shirts. There was no light after 6 p.m. The capital also saw military action. By 1945 Bangkok had been the target of more than 4,000 Allied air attacks, forcing the evacuation of 60 percent of the population.

Come Back Soon

In Thailand and Japan's Southern Advance 1940-1945, *E. Bruce Reynolds*

Events at the time of their repatriation in July and August 1942 alerted American and British diplomats to this Thai disenchantment with the Japanese. When it was learned that as a courtesy Ambassador Tsubokami had sent a parting gift of two cases of beer to [US] Minister Peck, the Thai Foreign Ministry, in a classic effort at one-upmanship, hastened to dispatch three cases to his ships. Phibun offered a gift of 70 baht to each of the repatriates, and he sent Minister Crosby a brief note expressing regrets and wishing him bon voyage.

Escape from Bangkok

From a letter written by Mrs. Mollie Dods to her family, detailing her escape with her husband, Samuel, from Bangkok to Rangoon in Dec. 1941.

We had just heard that the Japs had landed 20 miles away (further down the same road we lived in) and the Thais had been told not to resist.

We had a drink, collected our cases and went down to the British Club. It was dark by this time and practically a complete blackout out.

[Consul General] Crosby was already speaking. He explained the situation. Briefly, the Japs had invaded Malaya and we were at war with them. The Thais had given free passage of troops etc to Japan through Thailand. We were not at war with the Thais and there was no reason technically why any of us should not leave the country if we wanted to. But he went on as we all knew already, there was only one possible exit: by train to the North and across the border to Burma by car and lorry and it was not too easy a journey.

I think that at this point that I began to realise that we were pretty well trapped.

Mr Sargant [the head of Samuel's company] naturally would advise nobody. He said for his part he was waiting to see if the Legation Train would run and all our names were already down for it. But if any of the younger people (meaning certain young chaps who were here and certainly not Sam and I) wanted to have a shot at getting away, good luck to them.

One salesman who travelled and knew the country to a certain extent and spoke Thai well – then explained – vaguely. He said it would mean a long walk through the jungle at the end, anything up to 80 miles. I listened to all this and when we dispersed I said to Sargant, "I have no faith that the Legation will be able to do anything for us – I feel we should make some attempt." He answered rather dryly, "Even I could not walk through the jungle that distance, I am sure you couldn't." I answered, "I'd rather have a shot at it anyway if the alternative was to remain in Bangkok, which I felt it was."

That I am afraid was the last time I spoke to him. He waited along with the No 1 and 2 for the Legation Train, which never ran. They made an effort to get North on the Wednesday, but it was too late, some Japs arrested them at some station up the line.

War Crimes

Britain took the Thai declaration of war against the Allies much more seriously than the US and wanted to punish Thailand after Japan's surrender. But the Americans viewed Thailand as essentially an occupied country and forced London to drop some of its demands, which included abolishing the Thai armed forces and holding Thailand's military leadership accountable with war-crime trials. Given the decades of military dictatorship that followed (Phibul staged another coup just two years after the end of the war), many historians have wondered what would have happened if the British had gotten their way.

Cost of Living: Late 1941/Early 1942

First-class movie ticket at Chaloem Buri Cinema...10 satang (100 satang = 1 baht)
Monthly salary for a doctor...120 baht
Monthly salary for privates (Royal Thai Army or Police)...11.75-12 baht
Monthly rental of a wooden house...15 baht
Pair of combat boots...1.75 baht
Short time with a prostitute...75 satang
Ice coffee with fresh milk at Ui Lee Coffee Shop (the most famous in Bangkok)...6 satang
Meal for a family of four...50 satang
Phat Thai with an egg...6 satang
Bowl of noodles...5 satang
Rice with green curry and half a boiled egg...6 satang
Pack of Red Lion cigarettes (20 pieces)...8 satang
Source: Ajin Panjaphan

Thai Currency

Thai currency comes in denominations of 100 (red), 20 (green), 10 (reddishbrown), 5 (dark purple) and 1 (blue) Baht for printed notes and 50, 25, 10 and 5 Satang for coin fractions of a Baht.

Approximate Rates Given

CHEQUE WITH BANKS OR MONEY CHANGERS FOR DAY-TO-DAY RATES

CURRENCIES	Approximate Rates	
	Buying	Selling
Pound Sterling £	57.31	57.91
U.S. $	20.54 1/2	20.77
Hong Kong $	3.55 1/4	3.61 1/8
Singapore $	6.66 1/4	6.75 7/8
India Rupee	2.72	2.76 3/8

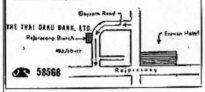
Conversion Table

U.S. DOLLARS INTO TICALS or BAHTS

RATE $	20.00	21.00	RATE $	20.00	21.00
1	20	21	51	1,020	1,071
2	40	42	52	1,040	1,092
3	60	63	53	1,060	1,113
4	80	84	54	1,080	1,134
5	100	105	55	1,100	1,155
6	120	126	56	1,120	1,176
7	140	147	57	1,140	1,197
8	160	168	58	1,160	1,218
9	180	189	59	1,180	1,239
10	200	210	60	1,200	1,260
11	220	231	61	1,220	1,281
12	240	252	62	1,240	1,302
13	260	273	63	1,260	1,323
14	280	294	64	1,280	1,344
15	300	315	65	1,300	1,365
16	320	336	66	1,320	1,386
17	340	357	67	1,340	1,407
18	360	378	68	1,360	1,428
19	380	399	69	1,380	1,449
20	400	420	70	1,400	1,470
21	420	441	71	1,420	1,491
22	440	462	72	1,440	1,512
23	460	483	73	1,460	1,533
24	480	504	74	1,480	1,554
25	500	525	75	1,500	1,575
26	520	546	76	1,520	1,596
27	540	567	77	1,540	1,617
28	560	588	78	1,560	1,638
29	580	609	79	1,580	1,659
30	600	630	80	1,600	1,680
31	620	651	81	1,620	1,701
32	640	672	82	1,640	1,722
33	660	693	83	1,660	1,743
34	680	714	84	1,680	1,764
35	700	735	85	1,700	1,785
36	720	756	86	1,720	1,806
37	740	777	87	1,740	1,827
38	760	798	88	1,760	1,848
39	780	819	89	1,780	1,869
40	800	840	90	1,800	1,890
41	820	861	91	1,820	1,911
42	840	882	92	1,840	1,932
43	860	903	93	1,860	1,953
44	880	924	94	1,880	1,974
45	900	945	95	1,900	1,995
46	920	966	96	1,920	2,016
47	940	987	97	1,940	2,037
48	960	1,008	98	1,960	2,058
49	980	1,029	99	1,980	2,079
50	1,000	1,050	100	2,000	2,100

Before 1860, cowry shells from the Maldives and bullet-shaped chunks of silver that weighed a "baht" (15.2 grams) were the main forms of currency. Hyper inflation hit the country in 1945 and after stability was restored the baht, or tical as it was also known, was pegged to the US dollar at about 20:1. "A tical is a nickel" was a favourite saying of American residents.

> "Ananda, the Siamese remember, was a strange young king. Full of Western ideas, he refused to talk to visitors who sat on the floor below him, Siamese fashion, insisting they sit on the chairs level with himself."
>
> TIME *magazine, 1950*

The King is Dead

An article from the Neue Zurcher Zeitung, *Apr. 15, 1950, describing the death of Ananda, King Rama VIII. Three palace employees were tried and executed for the crime, but it's widely believed that they were scapegoats. The secret of his tragic death will probably never be revealed.*

On the morning of June 9, 1946, news spread through the city that the king had been found in his bedroom with a bullet wound in his head. Was it an accident? Was it suicide or an assassination?

There were arguments for the three possibilities. There were people who maintained Ananda Mahidol had been apprehensive about the great responsibilities and colossal tasks awaiting him. Finally, suspicion was directed against a group of ambitious politicians whose supposed aim was the abolition of the monarchy[.]

> "The wound was caused by the king himself or it was caused by someone else."
>
> *Thai police department expert, after weeks of investigation*

P-Day at the Post

Alexander MacDonald, American spy and naval commander, reputedly arrived in Thailand aboard a US submarine before the Japanese surrendered in 1945. He remained to co-found the English-language Bangkok Post *with staff recruited from among Thais who had worked with him in the jungle and released Japanese prisoners with printing experience. After eight years as editor, MacDonald was ousted from the paper and Thailand by a military regime that opposed the* Post's *reporting. In the following passage, MacDonald describes the newspapers' first day, or "P-Day".*

I paced the press room, trying to round up enough front-page stories to make this first edition of the *Post* a newsy one. Little of note had come in over the wire services, so Page One would be made up entirely of local news.

Suddenly, *AP* reporter Stan Swinton dashed into the room. He didn't just arrive; that would not be Swinton. He rocketed into the office like Superman dropping in from a nearby planet. Attired in sweat-blotched khaki, he was a powerfully built young man, popping with energy.

"I'm Stanley Swinton of the *Associated Press*," he announced. "Call me Stan. Heard you were just getting started, and I've something for you. Just came in from the Indochina border, and all hell's breaking loose up there. French troops firing on Siamese towns. Saw it myself. How'd you like an eyewitness story?"

I sat him down at a typewriter. "String it out as long as you can, Stan," I told him.

Page 1 of the first edition of the Bangkok Post, August 1, 1946.

The Press Corps

From Mai Pen Rai Means Never Mind *by Carol Hollinger, 1950*

After meeting the correspondents and the men responsible for the stories in our most respected newspapers I regard everything in print as suspect. It isn't because I think I know more; I am simply aware of how little anybody knows. Behind the staid factual reports on South East Asia in the *New York Times* and the *London Times* I see now only the faces of the stringer correspondents who were my friends and I know where the news comes from. They do a good job...the best possible...and I am not criticizing, I am merely pointing out a complexity largely unrealized by the American public. You have to be God to distinguish truth from fiction in Thailand. And on second thoughts I think God might have difficulty unless he was Thai.

Like Kippling [sic] and the Dickens

Handbill for the Bangkok Times, *1906*

The news of English we tell the latest. Writ in perfectly style and most earliest. Do a murder git commit, we hear of it and tell it. Do a mighty chief die, we publish it, and in borders of sombre. Staff has each one been collaged, and write like the Kippling and the Dickens. We circle every town and extortionate not for advertisements. Buy it! Buy it! Tell each of you its greatness for good. Ready on Friday, Number first.

The Chinese Towkay

In People in a Native State *by J.H.M. Robson, 1894. Towkay (头家) was Hokkien for head of the household.*

After a time one discovers that there are a number of very good fellows among the Chinese, especially amongst those who bear the honoured prefix Towkay to their name. There is the mining Towkay, the contracting Towkay, the trading Towkay, the fishing Towkay, and a host of other little Towkays, in fact any Chinaman who has risen in the world called himself a Towkay.

Coming here as coolies under advances, never forgetting the birth-place and people they have left, with the speculative, practical, toiling attributes born within them, with nothing to lose and everything to gain, is it after all anything so very wonderful that some rise and blossom out into wealthy Towkays?

The personal peculiarities of a Towkay are not numerous; one appears to be that he must need let his nails grow to the length of an inch or more…This is an outward indication that the hands are not soiled by manual labour, but from personal observation I should imagine that this elongated little finger is kept as an — er — toothpick, say.

Another little peculiarity of my good friend, the Towkay, is the painful and audible habit he has of clearing his throat on arrival, during a conversation and even at meal times. He can hardly keep clock-work in his throat, but from the sounds one might suppose that about ten main springs had all broken at once, and he was doing his best not to swallow any of them.

Mild-mannered Reporter

Darrell Berrigan's courageous reporting in Burma during World War II, earning him fame and, it is suspected, a position in Bangkok with the OSS (the US spy agency that became the CIA). He was murdered – shot in the back of his car – in 1966. The police investigation was fruitless but subjected Bangkok's transvestite and homosexual community, with whom Berrigan was known to associate, to unprecedented scrutiny. He is described in this excerpt from TIME *magazine, July 21, 1958.*

The best daily newspaper in Thailand is edited by a wiry, wearily patient American named Darrell Berrigan. An expatriate newsman and long-time resident of Bangkok, Berrigan got his newspaper last year through an orientally inscrutable tactic – he wrote a magazine article charging that Thailand's chief cop, Gen. Phao Sriyanond, was also Thailand's biggest opium smuggler. General Phao was impressed. With characteristic Thai logic, he apparently reasoned that any newsman intimate enough with the country's boatmen, taxi drivers, prostitutes and businessmen to put together such a report would make an ideal editor. Phao hired Berrigan to edit his newly founded the *Bangkok World* – printed in English, because English is the second tongue of educated Thais and self-respecting Thai strongmen.

Phao was unceremoniously kicked out of the country in 1957. But before he left, he thoughtfully put aside funds – things are like that in Thailand – for Berrigan to keep going until he could scrape together enough money to buy control of the *World* for himself. Today Berrigan is such a national institution that diplomats phone him openly for guidance, and Thai officials consult him on politics – foreign and domestic. What is more, by his wit and wits, Editor Berrigan has turned his *World* into one of the genuinely cultured pearls of the East.

Wild Night at the Erawan

Kenneth Langbell's satire "Wild Night at the Erawan", first appearing in the 27 May 1967 **Bangkok Post,** *attracted worldwide infamy. Many readers of the later reprints believed the article was a real review.*

The recital, last evening in the chamber music room of the Erawan Hotel by U.S. pianist Myron Kropp...can only be described...as one of the most interesting experiences in a very long time.

A hush fell over the room as Mr. Kropp appeared from the right of the stage, attired in black formal evening-wear with a small white poppy in his lapel. With sparse, sandy hair, a sallow complexion and a deceptively frail looking frame, the man who has repopularized Johann Sebastian Bach approached the Baldwin Concert Grand, bowed to the audience and placed himself upon the stool...the Baldwin Concert Grand, while basically a fine instrument, needs constant attention, particularly in a climate such as Bangkok. This is even more true when the instrument is as old as the one provided in the chamber music room of the Erawan Hotel. In this humidity, the felts which separate the white keys from the black tend to swell, causing an occasional key to stick, which apparently was the case last evening with the D in the second octave.

During the "raging storm" section of the D-Minor Toccata and Fugue, Mr. Kropp must be complimented for putting up with the awkward D. However, by the time the "storm"

was past and he had gotten into the Prelude and Fugue in D Major, in which the second octave D plays a major role, Mr. Kropp's patience was wearing thin.

Some who attended the performance later questioned whether the awkward key justified some of the language which was heard coming from the stage during softer passages of the fugue. However, one member of the audience, who had sent his

children out of the room by the midway point of the fugue, had a valid point when he commented over the music and extemporaneous remarks of Mr. Kropp that the workman who had greased the stool might have done better to use some of the grease on the second octave D. Indeed, Mr. Kropp's stool had more than enough grease and during one passage in which the music and lyrics were both particularly violent, Mr. Kropp was turned completely around...

But such things do happen, and the person who began to laugh deserves to be severely reprimanded for this undignified behavior. Unfortunately, laughter is contagious, and by the time it had subsided and the audience had regained its composure Mr. Kropp appeared somewhat shaken. Nevertheless, he swiveled himself back into position facing the piano and, leaving the D Major Fugue unfinished, commenced on the Fantasia and Fugue in G Minor.

Why the concert grand piano's G key in the third octave chose that particular time to begin sticking I hesitate to guess. However, it is certainly safe to say that Mr. Kropp himself did nothing to help matters when he began using his feet to kick the lower portion of the piano instead of operating the pedals as is generally done.

Possibly it was this jarring or the un-Bach-like hammering to which the sticking keyboard was being subjected. Something caused the right front leg of the piano to buckle slightly inward, leaving the entire instrument listing at approximately a 35-degree angle from that which is normal. A gasp went up from the audience, for if the piano had actually fallen several of Mr. Kropp's toes if not both his feet, would surely have been broken.

It was with a sigh of relief therefore, that the audience saw Mr. Kropp slowly rise from his stool and leave the stage. A few men in the back of the room began clapping and when Mr. Kropp reappeared a moment later it seemed he was responding to the ovation. Apparently, however, he had left to get a red-handled fire ax which was hung back stage in case of fire, for that was what was in his hand.

My first reaction at seeing Mr. Kropp begin to chop at the left leg of the grand piano was that he was attempting to make it tilt at the same angle as the right leg and thereby correct the list. However, when the weakened legs finally collapsed altogether with a great crash and Mr. Kropp continued to chop, it became obvious to all that he had no intention of going on with the concert.

The ushers, who had heard the snapping of piano wires and splintering of sounding board from the dining room, came rushing in and, with the help of the hotel manager, two Indian watchmen and a passing police corporal, finally succeeded in disarming Mr. Kropp and dragging him off the stage.

Where Pleasure Is King

Bernard Kalb in The New York Times, *Apr. 15, 1961*

The mood of Bangkok is very special in Southeast Asia. Jakarta, the capital of Indonesia, for example, is a whirlpool of frustration, a capital in orbit around anti-colonial slogans. Singapore is energetic, engaged in a puritanical revolution. Kuala Lumpur in Malaya is easy-going, a capital with Arabian Nights architecture, where the work manages to get done every day. Bangkok, though is a rejuvenating tonic; the people seem to have found the magic elixir, Life, a visitor feels has not been wasted on the Thais.

Theirs is a land of joie de vivre where every moment seems worth celebrating.

Convivial gatherings for snacks, eight or nine times a day, are *sanouk* [joyful], and so are the kite-fights taking place at the Pramane Grounds. Gossiping is sanouk. So is television – "Mickey Spillane's Mike Hammer," dubbed in Thai, can be seen on Wednesday nights. A bottle of "Mekhong," the raw whisky made here, is "sanouk di," which is like saying "sanouk" twice.

HULA-HOOP

THE CRAZE THAT IS CIRCLING THE WHOLE WORLD

"Siam, as Asia goes these days, outwardly seems snug and insular, with that oddly idyllic quality that led British soldiers during the last war to dub it 'Toyland,' a parody on its new name, Thailand."

Life, *Feb. 20, 1950*

King Rama IX

When Bhumibol Adulyadej was born in Cambridge, Massachusetts, on Dec. 5, 1927, it seemed unlikely he would ever become king. The children of the reigning monarch (Prajadhipok) as well as Bhumibol's father (Mahidol) and elder brother (Ananda) all stood between him and the throne. Indeed, it took the *Bangkok Times* 10 days to report the royal birth in a couple of short sentences. Little did America realize that for the first and only time (so far), it would become the birthplace of a king.

Phibul's regime sought to marginalise the monarchy and for 25 years after Prajadhipok's abdication the country was effectively without a king, as Ananda and Bhumibol were children at the time of their respective accessions in 1935 and 1947. They both spent most of the 1940s in Swiss schools. King Rama IX, through his great personal charm, good works and political savvy, managed to restore the constitutional monarchy to the centre of Thai socio-political life.

"The Procession...ended the richly textured but extremely tiring ceremony for the king, a young man but not at all strong healthwise. Dressed in the uniform of the first monarch of the Chakri dynasty, wearing a warrior's hat with the brim turned up at one side, Bhumipol Adulyadej was carried on a palanquin by pages and accompanied by numerous soldiers dressed in traditional, colourful uniforms and armed with lances and spears."
–*Walter Bosshard in* Neue Zurcher Zeitung, *May 21, 1950*

Swingin' in the Reign

From TIME *magazine, July 1960*

NEW YORK: Last week King Bhumibol Adulyadej, who looks half his age, and his almond-eyed Queen Sirikit, who looks like mandolins sound, landed in Manhattan from Bangkok on their four-week swing through the U.S. And all the ticker-tape parade, the ride in the subway, the view from the Empire State Building faded into nothing when His Majesty went to dinner with the King of Swing, Benny Goodman (and 94 others) at the suburban estate of New York's Governor Nelson Rockefeller. For 90 minutes after dinner, the King and Benny led a foot-stomping, starch-melting jam session.

The King's romance with jazz is pleasantly tolerated by Queen Sirikit. For one thing His Majesty is monogamous, unlike most of his celebrated ancestors (his father was the 69th child of King Chulalongkorn). "He doesn't need any more wives," Queen Sirikit once said with a smile. "For him, his orchestra is one big concubine."

Take a plane
(Bobba doo zot)
Go to Siam...
In Bangkok
Today round the clock
Well, they all like to jam...
*"Now You Has Jazz," Bing Crosby
and Louis Armstrong, 1953*

A Dizzy Courtship

In Life, Feb. 20, 1950

It was music, in fact, that led to the king's engagement. Dining at the Siamese embassy in Paris two years ago, he met Princess Sirikit, then a budding 15-year-old with some odd ideas. For example, she had acquired a strong taste for bebop, The king, a confirmed anti-bebopist, argued patiently with her all through dinner but got nowhere. At the end he asked her father, Prince Mom Chao Nakkhatmongkhol Kitiyakara, for permission to take her out, let her listen to a few orchestras and discover what he meant. When the princess came to the Pensionnat Riante-Rive there were opportunities for more talk and personal demonstrations by the king on the piano. They never did settle the question, the princess holding firm on her bebopist convictions, but they did settle other things. Last July the king called Prince Nakkhatmongkhol to Lausanne, asked for the hand of his daughter.

Ruler of the Country

In The Associated Press, Apr. 22, 1950

The King is marrying Princess Sirikit next month, and like other Siamese he must sign the register.

Some government officials wanted his occupation listed as "King"; others objected. They wanted him listed simply as "Government Official".

After a long debate it was decided to describe the monarch as "Ruler of the Country".

Mystery of the Silk King

Jim Thompson's life was the stuff of novels – Princeton graduate, WWII station chief for the OSS, authority on Thai culture, friend and host to world leaders and movie stars. He took the fashion world by storm when his interest in the outstanding visual qualities of Thai silk inspired a Vogue *story that sparked worldwide interest in the material. His company remains one of Thailand's biggest and best silk producers, and his home is Bangkok's second-most-visited tourist attraction. But he's even better known for vanishing from the face of the Earth – or to be exact, from the jungle-clad Cameron Highlands of central Malaysia – while holidaying for Easter in 1967. A tourism business in the region has grown out of visitors attempting solve his fate, described as follows in a Cameron Highlands travel brochure.*

Thompson, previously a member of the CIA, disappeared mysteriously after going for an afternoon walk on…March 26th, 1967…the fact that he left his cigarettes and a small silver 'jungle box' on the chair outside Moonlight Cottage where he was staying suggests that he had not planned to be gone for long.

Thompson was never seen again.

Many believe he was kidnapped for his previous involvement in spying activities. However, it is more likely that he was eaten by a tiger, murdered in a botched robbery or fell into an aboriginal animal trap (a pit with a spike) and buried by [villagers]. Many hypotheses have been put forward to explain Thompson's disappearance…but what happened to him still remains one of the greater unsolved mysteries of Southeast Asia.

Jim Thompson – Alive in Cambodia?

From The New York Times, *Apr. 21, 1968.*

One group was certain from the very beginning that no ordinary fate had befallen the missing American. These were the *bomohs*, or witch doctors, of Malaysia, who entered the case early on.

From the first, all the *bomohs* have agreed that Thompson is still alive but they have differed considerably on exactly where and why. One said Thompson was in the hollow of a large tree, where he was being held by a disgruntled "Spirit of the Forest." Another announced the startling news that Thompson had been abducted by a blonde nightclub singer for obscure reasons and was in a jungle hut.

Toward the end of April the *bomohs* got some strong competition from a foreigner named Peter Hurkos, a Dutchman who claimed that a fall from a ladder had given him unusual powers of extrasensory perception. Friends in California recommended him to one of Thompson's sisters, who decided it was at least worth a try.

On his way to Bangkok, Hurkos and his attractive young assistant, Stephany Farb, stopped briefly in Hong Kong. Hurkos wanted to "check out" the Red Chinese border to see if he could "feel" anything. He felt nothing and proceeded to Thailand where he wanted to visit Thompson's house before going to the Highlands. There he had

some ominous feelings, especially in the dining room. Thompson, he announced, had been "playing with hot fire, associating with the wrong people." He talked with several of the missing man's friends, secured a recent photograph, and then left for the scene of the disappearance.

Moonlight Cottage provided a barrage of sensations. Holding the picture of Thompson in one hand and placing the other on maps of Southeast Asia and the Highlands area, Hurkos went into a kind of trance in which words seemed to tumble automatically out of his

mouth...this what he said happened: Thompson was sitting on the terrace alone. A man named Bebe or Preebie, came up and after shaking hands they walked down the road together. Bebe or Preebie was probably Thai. Half a mile down the road, the man put something on Thompson's face which caused him to go to sleep. Then a truck with 13 other men came along and the drugged man was taken in it to an airstrip in the jungle. From there he was flown to a village in Cambodia, where he was still being held captive.

When Hurkos returned to Bangkok with his story, there was a small diplomatic uproar. Among Thompson's political friends from the past was one named Pridi Phanomyong, who had several times served as prime minister of Thailand and who after a coup, had fled to Red China where as far as anyone knew, he was yet. The similarity between the ex-premier's name and the "Bebe or Preebie" that Hurkos "saw" was certainly striking. Furthermore, since neither Thailand

nor the United States had diplomatic relations with Cambodia and were in fact on very strained terms, the prospect of testing the kidnap theory was touchy indeed....it was decided not to make the test and Hurkos, professing disappointment, returned to the States suggesting before he left that he might take the matter up with President Johnson.

Age of the Dictators

From TIME *magazine, Sept. 1957*

For nearly 20 years the most agile, deft and eely politician in Southeast Asia's luxuriant political quagmire had been Thailand's steel-willed, soft-voiced dictator, Pibulsonggram. Westerners liked to dismiss Pibul as just another crooked politician. But he was much more than that. In many ways it was Pibul more than any other Thai leader who built modern Thailand...and in recent years he would say, "There are only three ways to remove a dictator: by exile, jail or burial."

Last week Pibul achieved exile. With him into discard, but in a different direction, went the more powerful of his two oldest and closest political cronies, Police Chief General Phao Sriyanond. His second long-time crony, Army Field Marshal Sarit Thanarat, stayed on in Bangkok, comfortably ensconced as the new political leader of Thailand.

Sarit added that he hoped Pibul would return, and "even run for Parliament, if he likes." Others were less kind. Cracked a Western diplomat: "This is the end of government of the Pibul, by the Pibul, and for the Pibul."

Time's Up, Prime Minister

In From Siam to Thailand: Backdrop to the Land of Smiles, *1982, Jorges Orgibet*
recounts witnessing Phibul's overthrow

I stepped out on the deck directly behind a naval officer waving an automatic weapon at the oncoming dignitaries. Marshal Phibul strode ahead to meet the gun-wielding officer. The PM was advised that he was under arrest. He acknowledged this information with a slight nod. He then glanced at the foot of the gangway where four armed naval ratings stood at the ready.

Gun-waved ashore, Phibul sauntered down the gangway. About midway, he turned and smilingly waved at the shocked dignitaries. The naval party herded Pibul to the south end of the Royal compound. He still refused to be hurried and walked slowly to the landing where he was escorted aboard a naval craft. As it moved up-river past the dredge, Phibul stood alongside the wheelhouse and waved again at the dignitaries.

The prime minister's captors brandished their weapons at the people on the dredge and virtually the entire diplomatic corps and their ladies hit the deck in their formal garb.

Hard Graft

From Economic Change in Thailand Since 1850 *by James C. Ingram, 1955*

Corruption is an extremely important phenomenon in the Thai economy, particularly in the period since World War II...Systematized "squeeze" and the routine "tea money," as found in Thailand, have become regular items of national income, and because of their location at strategic points in the government, they have great influence on the allocation of resources. This kind of bribery is found not only in government, but also in many levels of business...Corruption has economic importance because it introduces a new element of uncertainty into economic calculations. Whether a venture will succeed or fail may depend on one crucial "permit" or "special purchase," or it may depend on a succession of them...With the prospect of *total* failure always present, entrepreneurs must discount the future very heavily indeed. Fortunately, a kind of "standard" has developed even in corruption, and those who exceed the standard are (sometimes) exposed and punished.

"Coups have been a political way of life here for three decades. 'You have elections, we have coups,' a Thai once told a visitor."
American correspondent Bernard Kalb, Apr. 1961

Coup Season

"The King Signs Another Constitution", Associated Press, *1952*

King Bhumiphol Adulyadej today signed a new Thai Constitution backed by members of the military junta which overthrew the government in a bloodless coup d'etat nearly four months ago.

The king was on hand for elaborate presentation ceremonies promptly at 11 a.m. –the time deemed most auspicious by astrologers. Only yesterday Radio Bangkok announced officially that the ceremony had been postponed, but leaders of the military junta reportedly persuaded the king to change his mind. Field Marshall Sarit disclosed that at 11 p.m. Monday, General Thanom Kittikachorn, deputy army commander, met with the King. Asked what the King said about the army's seizure of power, Sarit replied: "What should the King say – everything was already finished."

Superlative Crook

The following is a tactful obituary from The New York Times, *Nov. 23, 1960, for Gen. Phao Sriyanond whom a respected Thai diplomat once described as the "worst man in the whole history of modern Thailand." Phao reportedly ran vice rackets, expropriated the profitable Bangkok slaughterhouse for himself, and rigged elections and the gold exchange. His influence stretched much further and was much darker – his National Police Force ran hit squads to eliminate political rivals, leftists, student activists, journalists, whistleblowers – anyone deemed a threat. The police force also organised the largest opium-trafficking syndicate in Thailand, rivalling that of the Thai military. For six years Phao, who was also the CIA's top client in Thailand, was recognised as the most powerful man in the country. He finally lost his grip on power following another military coup, and fled, with his sizeable fortune, to Swiss exile.*

Gen. Phao Sriyanond, former national police chief of Thailand, died yesterday of a heart attack at his home [in Switzerland]. He was 52 years old.

Gen. Phao (pronounced "Pow") was a colonel in the Thai army in 1947 when he helped to lead a coup that restored Field Marshal Pibul Songgram to power. After the success of the coup, Col. Phao was put in charge of the national police.

He eventually organized them into the strongest military force in the country, with 40,000 men, armored cars and even its own air force. Because of his connections, he was made director of many Thai businesses – 20 at one time – and was reportedly a wealthy man when sent into exile three years ago last September.

Model Strong Man

The US had initially viewed Sarit Thanarat as little more than a womanising drunkard before he proved his anti-communist credentials. After seizing power from Phibul and sending Phao, his other great rival, into exile, he ruled in a style that Suharto, Mobutu or Marcos would likely have appreciated. Sarit was in power for only five years (1958-63) before dying in office of cirrhosis. On his death, his assets were estimated at more than Bt2.8 billion, or about 30 percent of the total capital budget during his time in power. The government claimed about a quarter of it and the remainder was fought over by Sarit's 50 minor wives and their children.

Standoff in Lampang

From The Politics of Heroin in Southeast Asia *by Alfred McCoy, 1971*
The "opium war" between Phao and Sarit was a hidden one, with almost all the battles concealed by a cloak of official secrecy. The most comical exception occurred in 1950 as one of...Sarit's army convoys approached the railhead at Lampang in northern Thailand with a load of opium. Phao's police surrounded the convoy and demanded that the army surrender the opium, since antinarcotics work was the exclusive responsibility of the police. When the army refused and threatened to shoot its way through to the railway, the police brought up heavy machine guns and dug in for a fire-fight. A nervous standoff continued for two days until Phao and Sarit themselves arrived in Lampang, took possession of the opium, and escorted it jointly to Bangkok, where it quietly disappeared.

Fireman Politics

Jack Langguth in The New York Times,
Jan. 3, 1965

For a time, Thanom Kittikachorn tried copying some of the strong man's popular performances. Sarit had chased fire trucks and led police raids, so when fires broke out, Thanom appeared too. A Thai who has watched both men respond to alarm gave this report: "Sarit would arrive in his pyjamas, boots and fire hat. He'd be all over the scene – showing off, slapping firemen on the back. Sometimes he'd even shoot an arsonist right there on the spot. It was all very dishevelled – and with a fat man like Sarit very effective.

When Thanom tried it, he arrived in immaculate clothes and stood on one side. At every report that was brought to him he would smile – from nervousness, I think. He felt that he shouldn't be there; the appearances were getting unpopular so he stopped."

Bangkok Bombed

From the Wellington Evening Post, *Dec. 29, 1942*

A New Delhi communiqué states: "About midnight on Sunday a considerable force of our heavy bombers were over Bangkok, in Thailand, where various targets were effectively bombed.

"A large arsenal and powder factory north of the city was hit. The Bangkok aerodrome, one of the most important enemy fields in the occupied countries, was successfully attacked.

"At the same time, the naval dock area of the city was hit with heavy bombs which caused damaging fires. "None of our aircraft is missing."

Under the Stars Guiding Light

Life, *Nov. 21, 1949*

In happy little Siam – now officially called Thailand – people are more accustomed to coups d'état than they are to Coca-Cola. But Siam's coups and "Coke" have one thing in common. Neither can be launched successfully without the services of a reliable astrologer.

Last spring when William Dalton Davis, a young American, was about to introduce Coca-Cola in Bangkok, his Siamese associates called him aside. "We cannot open the new bottling works without consulting an astrologer," they told him flatly.

Davis was reluctant to let superstition interfere with business. But he tactfully consented, and three days later his partners returned grinning. "Operations can commence at 11.26 a.m. On April 8," they announced. "But that's a week early," Davis complained. "The plant won't be ready until the 15th."

"Then we must wait until 2:25 p.m. on May 12," they said.

"We can't afford to delay operations for a full month."

"If you refuse to take the astrologer's advice the Buddhist priests will refuse to bless the bottling machinery at opening ceremony," they persisted. "Then nobody in Siam will drink Coca-Cola."

On April 8, nine orange-robed Buddhist priests scurried barefoot through the gleaming new plant dabbing splotches of gold paint on bottling equipment and on Davis' forehead. At 11:26 a.m. the machinery was switched on.

People on the go
... go for Coke

In Thailand, it's ไทยไทย Mexicans call for ¡Si! Si.
In 81 countries around the globe, busy people refresh the pause for ice-cold Coca-Cola. It's the world's favorite way to refresh, for Coke gives a bit of quick energy ...and with so few calories as half an average, juicy grapefruit. No wonder Coke is the most asked-for soft drink in the world.

See EDDIE FISHER on "Coke Time" on TV. Television twice each week

Here Come the Americans

In the aftermath of World War II, the US became Thailand's main foreign patron. Washington poured funds into upgrading the country's ports, airports and national road system while aggressively promoting its "free enterprise" development model. Like China and the colonial powers before it, the US obtained preferential trading agreements for its own businessmen. Yet trade was always a secondary issue. Washington's main concern was strategic, based on Thailand's frontline status in the global struggle against communism. In pursuit of these interests, the US invested billions into strengthening Thailand's armed forces and supporting its military government.

In the early 1960s, with the Cold War turning decidedly hot in the region, Washington committed itself to protecting Thailand. In 1962, the US 7th Fleet was deployed in the Gulf of Thailand with 10,000 infantry sent to the Kingdom. More soldiers came in 1964 and by 1969 Thailand was host to 45,000 US military personnel.

Bangkok also allowed the US to operate a string of naval and air bases throughout the northern and eastern parts of the country. The first Thai-launched bombing strike on North Vietnam was carried out in December 1964. Thailand became known in Washington as the "unsinkable aircraft carrier", as three-quarters of the bomb tonnage dropped on Vietnam and Laos by the US during its war in Southeast Asia was flown from Thailand.

MISSION AND REASON FOR BEING IN THAILAND

Our assistance to the friendly governments of Southeast Asia has been of the highest importance in holding back the spread of communist inspired insurgency.

You represent the United States of America in helping our Southeast Asian friends to maintain an independent system in which the governments and their people can advance along history's long road without interference from the outside.

Freedom Fighters

From Thailand: The War That Is, the War That Will Be *by Louis E. Lomax, 1967*

"Your country must have lost all sense of moral commitment," a well-educated Thai said to me privately. "To use Thailand as a base to send bombers aloft in order to bring freedom to Viet Nam. If America is really committed to bringing freedom to Southeast Asia, you should start by bombing Bangkok!"

GIs in Bangkok

William Warren *in* The New York Times, *Aug. 7, 1966*

Since as everybody knows, military men have to have something to do in the evenings, the areas around the hotel billets (some of them in sedate residential sections) have been enlivened by the appearance of dozens of dim little bars bearing such descriptive names as the "Waiting for You," the "Why Not?," the "Sorry About That" and the simple but eloquent "Girl. Girl. Girl."

In addition there are a wide variety of massage parlours to choose from, ranging from small shady looking wooden houses on side streets to one plush air-conditioned establishment which brought out a special newspaper supplement to celebrate its grand opening. Lithe beautiful masseuses in attendance, management promised, would wear "topless semi-bikinis" while performing their chores and went on to explain: "Halters aren't practical since they come off in the washing process anyway."

"The city's rich colours and smells and sounds were an intoxicant that liberated the libido; everyone in Bangkok seemed to be living on a hot tin roof."

Kiwi journalist Peter Arnett describing his 1958 arrival

151

US Army Master Sergeant Ike Atkinson leveraged his deployment in Bangkok to build one of the largest heroin smuggling rings out of Southeast Asia. Rumours that Atkinson had smuggled drugs in the body bags of US servicemen took on the power of an urban myth but no evidence of this was ever established. Atkinson himself denied it. Atkinson was also an investor in one of the first bars to cater for African-American GIs in Bangkok, in 1967.

The English word "Butterfly" is used in Thai bar areas as a term for promiscuous men. It was, according to some accounts, not a direct import from the West, but introduced by the Japanese during their WWII occupation. The word derives from the 15-year-old Japanese Geisha nicknamed Cho-Cho (Butterfly) who marries an American sailor in Puccini's opera "Madame Butterfly". The Japanese also introduced the bar-beer/go-go bar word "mama-san", meaning the "big boss".

For the Economic Good

In 1968, Fred Poole, a Time Life *correspondent, attended a press conference given by Gen. Prapas Charusathira, a member of the triumvirate that held power under Field Marshal Thanom Kittikachorn. Poole recounted the conference in* Bangkok After Dark, *which he wrote in 1968 under the pseudonym Andrew Harris.*

Reporter: It has often been said that the number of bars and massage parlors contributes to juvenile delinquency. What do you think, sir?

Prapas: That's not true. We need more of this kind of service.

Reporter: We have also heard that it's detrimental to the economy and making everyone a spendthrift.

Prapas: That's not right. These places are good for the country economically. Bars, nightclubs and massage parlors are for farangs (caucasians) who can afford such services. You can avoid being a spendthrift by avoiding such places, like I do…

Reporter: Do you think marriages between Thai girls and farangs should be registered in embassies?

Prapas: There is no need to register in the embassy. It is far easier to go to the district office and register by paying a fee. But this is a minor matter. I have not heard of many cases. Many of the couples find an easier way out, or so I have been told by an American friend. They go to hotels or motels and when the farang is asleep the girl "swipes" him clean, pants and all.

Loose Lips

From The New York Times, *June 23, 1966*

"Button Your Lip," the United States Air Force's weekly *Klong Times* today told its readers among 18,000 United States airmen stationed in Thailand... American officials here have become worried and exasperated by the evidence that happy-go-lucky servicemen on leave from Vietnam or key air bases in Thailand talk too much in Bangkok's crowded bars and noisy cabarets about their work.

Who's listening? Probably not the bored Thai hostess, but quite likely, United States sources say, a sharp young fellow from the Soviet embassy.

The Russians and their Thai helpers have taken to spending time in the off-duty haunts of American servicemen.

For example, near the riverfront Oriental Hotel, young English-speaking Russians have been noticed eaves-dropping on, and even joining, the bar conversations of friendly enlisted men at the Drop In cabaret and other establishments.

The nightclub area is favored by members of the Special Forces, the U.S. army's anti-guerrilla specialists, and by pilots of the secrecy-shrouded Air America, the Central Intelligence Agency's airline which makes mysterious flights into Thailand, Laos and Vietnam.

"We tell everybody to shut up," a United States official said in discussing the situation. "But you know Americans – Yak, yak, yak."

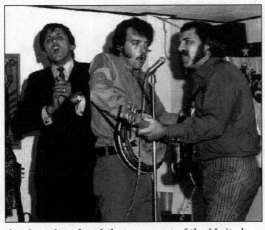

An American band that was part of the United Service Organisation (USO)

"Thailand's Deputy Premier declared today that the off-duty behavior of some of the 37,000 United States soldiers in this country was 'disgusting.' He said he was particularly upset by the way the soldiers carried on in public with Thai women."

UPI, *Apr. 13, 1967*

Boys Will Be...Girls

Descriptions of "lady boys" and the difficulty in telling them apart from "real women" are now a staple of tourists' recollections from a trip to Thailand, but such tales are a relatively new phenomenon. In contrast, early visitors to Bangkok were far more likely to comment on how masculine the crop-haired local women looked as opposed to how effeminate some of the men may have appeared. The prevalence of cross-dressing men today is usually attributed to Thailand's generally tolerant culture and a rural tradition of transvestite beauty contests. The use of the Thai term *kathoey* for certain homosexual men is thought to date back several centuries, although it is really only in the last 30 years that it has come to be closely associated with men in high heels and short dresses. The availability of women's hormone-based contraceptives and sex-change operations in the last few decades has further supported the trend by making it easier for men to take the appearance of women.

The Big Switch

From The Nation, *July 1972*

A team of doctors from Ramathibodi Hospital attempted Thailand's first known sex-change operation and after five hours of surgery they claimed success – they had transformed a man into a woman, complete with a female sexual organ...Dr. Vichit Bunyahotra, said the operation had been carefully planned since the beginning of the year so that the patient, formerly Mr. Lek Hokkam, who had been living with an American serviceman stationed in Udon Thani, would be ready for the sex change...The preparations included periodic injections of female hormones to ensure Lek's body would not suffer too abrupt a change when his male organ, which produced male hormones, was removed during the operation.

The doctor said he foresaw no legal complications in obtaining a new legal status for Lek. "We are going to issue a certificate that will help him register his new status," he said.

Land of Smiles

The Law of the Three Seals encoded under Rama I defined a prostitute as little different from an adulteress – as a woman who has sex with more than one man in the course of a day. Money and sex, the implication seemed to be, were entwined. In the 1800s, the large pool of male immigrant workers from China fueled demand for prostitution in Bangkok, and by the end of the century there were a small number of brothels, hotels and all-night bars established in and around the Bangrak area adjacent to the Chao Phraya River – also where most of the foreigners lived. Among these establishments were about eight European bar/brothels, most of which were staffed by Russian women, along with a few Germans and Italians.

From the late 19th century, the scale of prostitution increased dramatically as the city developed. One source estimated that in the post-WWII years there were 85 cabarets scattered across the city with names like Great World, Happy World, Venus Club and – recalling the glories of Sampheng – the Green Lantern. The greatest concentration was not far from today's red-light area at Patpong, on a block of Nares Road, where an estimated 2,000 "hostesses" worked.

Cabarets

In From Siam to Thailand *by Jorges Orgibet, 1982*

The cabarets were a direct descendant of the Thai ramwong dances found in almost every town and at every fair. Live shows, blue movies, young virgins were touted by rickshaw pullers and bicycle samlor drivers long before the touts of Patpong and Petchburi came into existence... It was 300,0000 Japanese troops during World War II...and the 30,000 British and Indian troops who followed them that helped fill Bangkok's cabarets.

The Pious Madam

Yai Faeng was the queen of early Bangkok's brothel and opium den district in Sampheng. The girls at her brothel in Yannawa's Tao Alley were known for their beauty and refinement, their colourful Thai and Chinese dresses and the flowers in their hair. Yai Faeng was also a devout Buddhist and funded the construction of a temple in 1833. It quickly became known as Wat Mai Yai Faeng (Temple of Grandmother Faeng) – probably the world's only house of worship in the world named after a brothel owner. Her statue can still be seen beside a wall in the backyard of the ordination hall. Yai Faeng's descendants renovated the monastery and asked King Rama IV to give it a new name. He settled upon Wat Khanika Phon, a mix of Pali and Thai meaning "The temple built from the profits of the prostitute".

Miss Pretty Girl

Somerset Maugham, recounting a card given to him by a tout he met on the streets of Bangkok, in The Gentleman in the Parlour, *1930.*

Oh, gentleman, sir, Miss Pretty Girl welcome you to Sultan Turkish Bath, gentle polite massage, put you in dreamland with perfume soap. Latest gramophone music. Oh, such service. You come now! Miss Pretty Girl want you, massage you from tippy-toe to head-top, nice, clean, to enter Gates of Heaven.

157

Underworld Theatre

In From Golden Gate to Golden Sun *by Hermann Norden, 1923*

We had paddled about a mile downstream (Chao Phrya) before we boarded a raft, on which a square, wooden house was built. This house proved to be a theatre of the underworld. By the light of a kerosene lamp, we bought tickets at twenty satangs each (eight US cents). Smoke obscured the view as I entered, but when my eyes grew accustomed, I thought I must have strayed by mistake into a public bath. I seemed to be surrounded by naked arms and legs, naked shoulders, naked bosoms, much jewelry and a few gay shawls.

I did not linger. The noise, smoke and generally hideous atmosphere stifled any desire to extend my studies...I only wanted to get out of that hellish place.

The Bolero

The action in Jack Reynolds' classic 1956 novel A Woman of Bangkok *centres on a bar called the Bolero, which many old timers insist was based on an open-air dance hall called The Cathay.*

It's a weird place the Bolero. It's like a share-cropper's shanty on Brobdingnagian scale. A raised wooden floor, acres in extent; no walls; a low gloomy roof. From the gloom hang dozens of tawdry paper lanterns, all very dim and dusty. In the middle of the floor is a circular space waxed for dancing; this is flanked by rows of tiny desks at which girls sit like amazingly exotic schoolgirls in kindergarten. The rest of the place is strewn with wicker armchairs arranged in fours around small tables. There is a bar of sorts and a band, also of sorts. Prices are fantastically high. Beer costs 10 bob a bottle instead of the normal Bangkok price of six. The girls are said to be expensive too. Certainly the famous ones Frost said were remembered with nostalgia from Greenland's icy mountains to India's immoral strand, wherever men of itchy feet and another irritating itch silt up bars for an hour or so before the next hop.

Live Show! Live Show!

The influx of GIs during the
Vietnam War may have encouraged
sex shows, but this type of
entertainment had already emerged
as a feature of Bangkok nightlife
by the early 1920s. A report in the
popular newspaper from the era,
Sayam Rat, described how employees
from the *Chai-oi ngiw* (Chinese
folk opera) walked around the city
streets carrying placards advertising
performances of a "humorous tale
with interesting pornographic
elements". The campaign drew
large crowds, primarily from the
Chinese community, to see a show
that featured young male and female
performers on stage. According
to the newspaper, the show began
with the two protagonists admiring
scenery in a garden, flirting with
another and then "falling in love".
As the story unfolds, the performers
stripped down and then proceeded
to simulate copulation in a most
"realistic fashion" before a packed
audience who "cheered them on
enthusiastically".

"These women are meretricious,
avaricious, mendacious and bone
lazy. Never give your heart to a
demimondaine: she'll chew it up
and spit it out."
Bernard Trink, Bangkok World *and*
Bangkok Post *columnist (1962-
2003)*

To Serve and Protect

From Bangkok After Dark *by Andrew Harris (Fred Poole), 1968*

The attitude of the police to Bangkok's after-dark activities is perhaps best summed up by a statement released not long ago to the press. The officer issuing the statement noted that tourists had been complaining about being molested by streetwalkers. He advised the tourists to have nothing to do with streetwalkers, and pointed out that the police were always ready to be of assistance. He said that any tourist was welcome to drop in at any police station, where he could pick up a list of safe and respectable prostitutes.

Patpong

Probably no 120-meter stretch of Thai land is better known than Patpong. While the arrival of GIs is widely held as the catalyst for its evolution into one of the world's best-known red-light districts, the true story is a little different. Developed as a row of shophouses in the 1950s by the Patpongpanit family (who still own the land), the area attracted foreign businesses such as airlines, shipping companies, news agencies, and even the US Information Service, thanks to a revolutionary rental arrangement at the time – higher monthly rents in lieu of a large deposit. By 1968, a handful of nightclubs that gained a reputation for offering "foreigner friendly services" had sprung up in the lane and a legend of sorts was born. During the Vietnam War years, Patpong served as a rest-and-recuperation location for U.S. troops. In its prime during the 1970s and 1980s, Patpong became famous for its bikini-clad go-go dancers and sexually explicit shows. In recent years, the strip has lost some of its harder edge, with merchants hawking pirated goods crowding out their brothers from the more traditional night services trade.

The Third Sex

In one of the first press accounts of a partial cross-dresser in Bangkok, Nai Lert, writing in the July 18, 1924 edition of Bangkok Kanmeuang, *describes a young man who apparently aspired to be a "beauty queen," parading on the streets of the capital.*

Oh, dear goddess! He was wearing light pink silk trousers and a pale green silk shirt. On his left wrist was a watch, on his right wrist a bracelet, and he wore a necklace around his neck.

The Thai Ideal

MR Kukrit Pramoj, an English-educated aristocrat, served as a sort of cultural translator for the West through his writings and public duties (he even played the part of the prime minister of a fictional Asian country opposite Marlon Brando in "The Ugly American".) In a 1987 interview with an American reporter he explained:

"The Thai ideal is an elegant sort of life, with adaptable morals and a serene detachment to the more serious problems of life."

"Your salary is small – at least the part that is paid out here is – and that's for a sound reason. It gives you enough to have a good time on, but not enough to have too good a time on."

Jack Reynolds, 1956

Teacher, Student

From Carol Hollinger's Mai Pen Rai Means Never Mind, *1950*

At first I thought smugly that I was bringing democratic freedom of speech to a group that knew only oligarchy and dictatorship, but as the classroom discussions deepened I found with enforced humility (I was clobbered) that somehow I had become the learner and my students were on the pedagogic end.

161

Lovable Bangkok

In Bangkok: Story of a City, *Alec Waugh writing about Bangkok after spending decades away.*

No place remains the same for ever. But Bangkok has been loved because it is the expression of the Thais themselves, of their light heartedness, their love of beauty, their reverence for tradition, their sense of freedom, their extravagance, their devotion to their creeds – to characteristics that are constant and continuing in themselves. Bangkok has always been that; I think that it will stay that way; I do not believe it can be spoiled.

"When all is said and done, Bangkok remains an unusually pleasant city – because of the people. The Thais are 60 per cent literate, 90 percent Buddhist, and 100 percent obliging."
Journalist Jack Langguth,
Jan. 3, 1965

"Go home soon; otherwise you won't want to."
Belgian jurist Emile Jottrand,
writing in 1898, offered the following
advice to new arrivals.

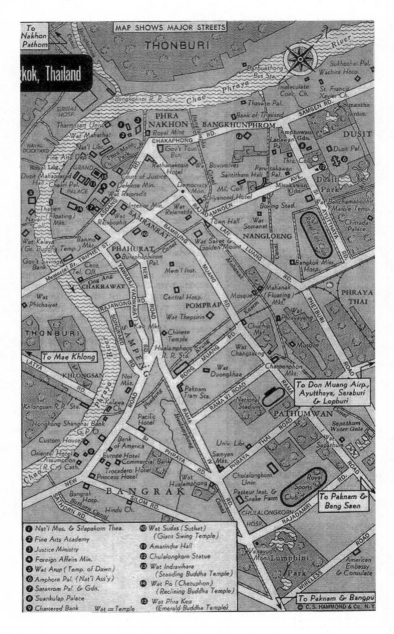

Bibliography

John Anderson, *English Intercourse with Siam in the 17th Century*, 1830 (Reprint: Lightning Source Inc, 2007)

Antonio, J., *The 1904 Traveller's Guide to Bangkok and Siam* (Reprint: White Lotus Press, 1997)

Arnett, Peter, *Live From the Battlefield*. New York: Touchstone, 1995

Associated Press, Apr. 22, 1950

Bacon, George, *Siam, The Land of the White Elephant, As It Was and Is*. New York: C. Scribner's Sons, 1892.

Baker, Chris and Phongpaichit, Pasuk, *A History of Thailand*. London: Cambridge University Press, 2009.

"Bangkok Bombed", *Wellington Evening Post*, Dec. 29. 1942

"Bangkok Expats Mourn Thermae Closure", *UPI*, July 12, 1996

Barmé, Scot, *Woman, Man, Bangkok: Love Sex and Popular Culture in Thailand*, Lanham, MD: Rowman and Littlefield, 2002

Besso, Salvatore, *Siam and China*, London: Simpkin, Marshall, Hamilton, Kent & Co., Ltd, 1914

Blofeld, John, *King Maha Mongkut of Siam*, Singapore: Asia Pacific Press, 1972

Bock, Carl, *Temples and Elephants*, 1881 (reprint by White Lotus Press, Bangkok, 1985)

Boshard, Walter, "Coronation of a King", *Neue Zurcher Zeitung*, May 21, 1950

Bowring, Sir John, *The Kingdom and People of Siam*, 1830, (reprint by Oxford University Press, Kuala Lumpur, 1969)

British Chamber of Commerce, *Life in Early Bangkok*, 2010

Beauvoir, Ludovic, marquis de, *A Week in Siam*, Jan. 1867: Siam Society, 1986

Bradley, Dr. Daniel Beach, *The Bangkok Recorder*, 1844

Bradley, Dr. Daniel Beach, *Bangkok Calendar 1862*, American Missionary Association, 1862

Buls, Charles, *Siamese Sketches* (1901), translated by Walter E. J. Tips. Bangkok: White Lotus, 1994.

Bulwer-Lytton, Baron Edward, *The Siamese Twins: A Satirical Tale of our Times. With Other Poems*, 1831

Burton, William, writing in *The New York Times*, Aug. 29, 1937

Campbell, J.G.D., *Siam in the Twentieth Century, Being the Experiences and Impressions of a British Official*. London: E. Arnold, 1902

Child, Jacob T. (US ambassador) *The Pearl of Asia*. Chicago: Donohue,

Henneberry & Co., 1892

"Chinese Riots", *Bangkok Times*, July 20, 1889

Conrad, Joseph, *The Shadow Line; A Confession*, J. M. Dent & Sons (Wordsworth Editions, 1998)

Conrad, Joseph, Lord Jim, J. M. Dent & Sons (Wordsworth Editions 1998)

Conrad, Joseph, *Youth*, 1888

Crawfurd, John, *Journal of an Embassy from the Governor-General of India*, 1827, London: Henry Colburn and Richard Bentley, 1830

Daniels, W.B., *Siamese Twins: Some Observations on Their Life, Last Illness and Autopsy*, 1963

Earl, George Windsor, *The Eastern Seas*. London: W.H. Allen & Co, 1837

"Education In Siam; A Normal College Opened In Bangkok". *The New York Times*, Aug. 14, 1879

"Energetic Action of the Consul at Bangkok in Closing Spirit Shops". *The New York Times*, Aug. 17, 1878

Farrington, Anthony, *Siam in Early Missionaries in Bangkok: The Journals of Tomlin, Gutzlaff and Abeel*, 1828–1832, Bangkok 2001

Fineman, Daniel, *A Special Relationship: The United States and Military Government in Thailand*. University of Hawaii Press, 1997

"Flight of the Thunderbird". *TIME*, Sept. 30, 1957

"For Westerners the Good Life", *Life*, Dec. 31, 1951

Fournereau, Lucien, *Bangkok in 1892*, translated by Walter E.J. Tips. Bangkok: White Lotus Press, 1998.

Freeman, Andrew, *Brown Women and White*, New York: John Day, 1932

"Garden of Smiles". *TIME*, April 3,1950

Gervaise Nicolas, *The Natural and Political History of the Kingdom of Siam* (1690), Reprint. Bangkok: White Lotus Press, 1998.

W. J. Gedney, Phaya Anuman Rajadhon, *Life and Ritual in Old Siam: Thai Life and Customs*. New Haven Greenwood Press, 1961

"The Giant Swing", article, *Bangkok and Siam Directory*, 1914

Gorer, Geoffrey, *Bali and Angkor*. London: Michael Joseph: 1936

Harris, Andrew (Fred Poole), *Bangkok After Dark*. New York: Macfadden-Bartell, 1968

Harris, Townsend, *The Complete Journal of Townsend Harris*, 1856. New York: Macmillan, 1914

Hollinger, Carol, *Mai Pen Rai Means Never Mind*. Boston: Houghton Mifflin, 1965

Hughes, Richard, *The Wall Street Journal*, Feb. 26, 1959

Eileen Hunter, *Narisa Chakrabongse (M. R.) Katya & the Prince of Siam*, River Books, 1994

"In Memory of the State Visits of His Majesty the King: The Royal Compositions of Her Majesty Queen Sirikit", *Bangkok Post*, Oct. 2004

Ingram, James, *Economic Change in Thailand Since 1850*. Kuala Lumpur: Oxford University Press, 1955

"Is Jim Thompson Alive and Well in Asia?". *The New York Times*, April 21, 1968

Jackson, Peter, "Tolerant but Unaccepting: The Myth of a Thai Gay Paradise", in: Peter Jackson and Nerida Cook (eds), *Genders and Sexualities in Modern Thailand*, Chiangmai: Silkworm Books (1999)

Jennings' Guide to Singapore, Penang, Malacca, Johore, Deli, Bangkok, etc. (1900) (Archive.org)

Jottrand, Emile, *In Siam: The Diary of a Legal Adviser* (1905) translated by White Lotus Press, 1995

"The King Signs Another Constitution", *Associated Press*, Mar. 8, 1952

Kirkup, James, *In Cities of the World: Bangkok*. London: Littlehampton Book Services, 1968

Kornerup, Ebbe, *Friendly Siam*, translated from the Danish by M. Guiterman. London, New York, G. P. Putnam's Son, Ltd, 1928

Leonowens, Anna, *The English Governess at the Siamese Court*, [1870] (Singapore: Oxford University Press, 1988)

Leonowens, Anna, *The Romance of the Harem*, 1850 (Singapore: Oxford University Press, 1988

Leonowens, Anna, Anna Leonowens' Experiences in the Siamese Court: The Atlantic Monthly, 1870

"Letter: Chasing the Dragon", *Bangkok Times*, Mar. 14, 1923

Lomax, Louis, *Thailand: The War That Is, the War That Will Be*. New York: Random House, 1967

Loti, Pierre, *Siam*. York, Frederick A. Stokes company 1930

McCoy, Alfred, *The Politics of Heroin in Southeast Asia*, 1971

Alexander MacDonald, *My Footloose Newspaper Life*. Bangkok: Post Publishing, 1990

Marshall, Thomas William, *In Christian Missions: Their agents, and Their Results*, 1864

Matichon newspaper, special edition, "History of Agricultural Technology", 2005

Maugham, Somerset, *The Gentleman in the Parlour*. London: William

Heinemann Ltd, 1930

Miller, Thomas, *Over Five Seas and Oceans, from New York to Bangkok, Siam, and Return: Some Reminiscences*. New York: A. Metz, 1893.

Montgomery, Bob, "Prince Anonymous", *The Irish Times*, 1985

"Old Orient Hand". *TIME*, July 21, 1958.

Paul Morand, *Rien que la Terre*. Paris. B, Gasset, 1926

Henri Mouhot, *Travels in the Central Parts of Indo-China* (Siam, Cambodia, and Laos, during the Years 1858, 1859, and 1860). London, John Murray, 1864.

Neale, Frederick Arthur, *Narrative of a Residence at the Capital of the Kingdom of Siam*, 1840, (reprint: Bangkok: White Lotus, 1997)

North-China Herald, 31 October 1925

Norden, Hermann, *From Golden Gate to Golden Sun: a Record of Travel, Sport and Observation in Siam and Malaya.*, London: H. F. & G. Witherby, 1923.

Orgibet, Jorges, *From Siam to Thailand*. Bangkok: Kofco, 1982.

The Otago Witness (New Zealand), 1894

Pallegoix, Bishop Jean-Baptiste, *Grammatica Lingua Thai, and Description, i.* 1850, (reprint Bangkok: White Lotus 2000)

Pallegoix, Jean-Baptiste, *Description du Royaume Thai ou Siam: comprenant la topographie, histoire*, 1840, (1854, Reprint: Bangkok, White Lotus, 2000)

Ajin Panjaphan, *My Country Thailand: Its History, Geography and Civilization*, 1942

"P-Day at the Post", *Bangkok Post*, Aug. 1, 1946

Philadelphia Medical Times, 1874

Powell, E. Alexander, *Where the Strange Trails Go Down*, 1921. Project Gutenberg

"Premier Sarit, 55, Dies In Thailand". *The New York Times*, Dec. 8, 1958

Reid, Eric, Chequered Leaves from Siam, Bangkok: Bangkok Times Press, 1913 (Archive.org)

"Revolt of the Triads", *Bangkok Times*, July 20, 1889

Reynolds, Bruce, *Thailand's Secret War: The Free Thai, OSS, and SOE*. London, Cambridge University Press, 2005

Reynolds, Jack, *Woman of Bangkok*, Ballantine Books, 1968. (First published 1956)

Robert, Dr Leopold, Venereal Diseases in Siam 1922, League of the Red Cross Societies, Far Eastern Conference, Bangkok, November-December, 1922

Rolin-Jaequemyns, Gustave, *Gustave Rolin-Jaequemyns and the Making of Modern Siam: The Diaries and Letters of King Chulalongkorn's General Adviser*. translated by Walter Tips, Bangkok 1996.

Rolnick, Harry, *Flavours: Thailand's 200 Most Interesting Restaurants*. Bangkok: Siam Communications, 1972

Ruschenberger, W.S.W. *A Voyage Round the World: Including an Embassy to Muscat and Siam in 1835, 1836, and 1837*. London: R. Bentley, 1838.

"Siam: Return of Phibun". *TIME*, Nov. 24, 1947

"Siam True To Orient". *The New York Times*, Aug. 29, 1937

"Smiling Through With Thanom of Thailand". *The New York Times*, Jan. 3, 1965

Smith, Malcolm, *A Physician at the Court of Siam*. (1910) (Reprinted: Kuala Lumpur, Oxford University Press, 1982)

Smith, Nicol, *Into Siam: Underground Kingdom*. Indianapolis: Bobbo Merrrill Co., 1946

Smithies, Michael, *Alexander Hamilton: A Scottish Sea Captain in Southeast Asia, 1689-1723*, (Silkworm Books)

Smyth, H. Warington, *Five years in Siam, from 1891 to 1896*. New York: Scribner, 1898.

"Some Bright Phases of Oriental Life". *The New York Times*, July 4, 1901

Spokane Daily Chronicle, 30 April 1932

The Stars Rule Siam, *Life*, Nov. 21, 1949

The Straits Times, 3 October 1905

"Swingin' in the Reign". *TIME*, July 18, 1960

Tailor and Cutter magazine, 1892

"The Most Beautiful Word in English? Bangkok Says, 'Progress' ". *The New York Times*, Aug. 7, 1966

Tomlin, Jacob, *Journal of Nine Months' Residence in Siam*. London: Frederick Westley and AH Davis, 1831 (Google Books)

UPI, April 13, 1967

"US Servicemen in Bangkok Are Urged to Be Tactfully Silent". *The New York Times*, June 24, 1966

Vincent, Frank, *The Land of the White Elephant: Sights and Scenes in Southeastern Asia*. (1871) (Kessinger Publishings Legacy Repeat Series 2004)

Warren, William, *Bangkok*. London: Reaktion Books, 2002

Warren, William, *Jim Thompson: the Unsolved Mystery*, Archipelago Press, 1998

Waugh, Alec, *Bangkok: The Story of a City*, 1971 (White Lotus Co.1990.)

"Wild Night at the Erawan", *Bangkok Post*, May 27, 1967

Prince Wilhelm of Sweden, *In the Lands of the Sun: Notes and Memories of a Tour in the East*. E. Nash, 1915

Wood, W.A.R., Land of Smiles, Bangkok, Krungdebarnagar Press, 1935

Wyatt, David K., *Thailand, A Short History*. Yale University Press, 2003
Young, Ernest, *The Kingdom of the Yellow Robe*. London: Archibald Constable & Co, 1898
"Young King With a Horn", *Life*, Feb. 20, 1950
Younghusband, G.J., Journey Across Central Asia. Proceedings — Royal Geographical Society, 1888